Lawmaking and the Legislative Process

W9-CAB-833

Lawmaking and the Legislative Process
Committees, Connections, and Compromises

by Tommy Neal

National Conference of State Legislatures

ORYX PRESS
1996

The rare Arabian Oryx is believed to have inspired the myth of the unicorn. This desert antelope became virtually extinct in the early 1960s. At that time several groups of international conservationists arranged to have 9 animals sent to the Phoenix Zoo to be the nucleus of a captive breeding herd. Today the Oryx population is over 1,000, and 500 have been returned to the Middle East.

© 1996 by the National Conference of State Legislatures
Published by The Oryx Press
4041 North Central at Indian School Road
Phoenix, Arizona 85012-3397

Published simultaneously in Canada
Printed in the United States of America

∞The paper used in this publication meets the minimum requirements of American
National Standard for Information Science—
Permanence of Paper for Printed Library Materials,
ANSI Z39.48, 1984

Library of Congress Cataloging-in-Publication Data
Lawmaking and the legislative process: committees, connections, and
compromises / by Tommy Neal
    p.   cm.
Includes bibliographical references and index.
ISBN 0-89774-944-8 (paper)
    1. Legislation—United States—States.   2. Bill drafting—United
States—States.   3. Legislative bodies—United States—States—
Committees.   I. National Conference of State Legislatures.
KF4945.Z9L39   1996
328.73'0773—dc20   96-20568
                                                          CIP

CONTENTS

• • • • • • • • •

PREFACE

· · · · · · · · ·

For many of us, the process of lawmaking, in general and as it relates to our personal lives, is mysterious and, oftentimes, incomprehensible. Knowledge of the legislative process, however, is essential to our developing an appreciation of the civic and governmental structure of the United States.

A major purpose of this book, therefore, is to shed light on the mysteries of lawmaking and the workings of legislatures, particularly state legislatures, as they continue to assume a more important role in our federal system.

This book was originally intended for high school and junior college students, as they begin to discover how the government under which they live is structured. But we believe that this resource also serves as a refresher source for those who may want to brush up on their understanding of how laws are made, especially where the similarities and differences between the state and federal legislative processes are concerned. Although many of the illustrative examples found in these pages are geared toward young people, these examples were all chosen because their relevance extends to every citizen of the United States, whether young or old.

In exploring the lawmaking process at the state level, we have utilized fictional characters, who sponsor a variety of bills, and we follow their proposals through the legislative process. The sample bills that are included in the text are based on the bill format of the Colorado legislature. It should be noted that every state has its own version of the format of bills—no two are alike.

And, as with bill format, each of the nation's 50 state legislatures is unique in its method of operation and in its lawmaking process. There are numerous similarities but no constants, a point that is made throughout the text. Readers, therefore, who are interested in participating in state government will need to carefully examine the legislative process in their own states.

Lawmaking is not confined to state legislatures, of course, and so we have included information concerning the U.S. Congress, using a case study of major legislation—the omnibus crime bill enacted by Congress in 1994—as well as information on the organization, process, and role of local governments in making laws and providing services. Also included is information about the initiative, referendum, and recall devices, which give citizens in many states an opportunity to participate directly in making laws and recalling elected officials.

Another major purpose of the book is to encourage readers to make the connections that are essential to an understanding of our federal system of government. Public opinion polls reveal that the general public fails to make connections between the various levels of government that affect their daily lives, confusing, for example, state legislators with members of the U.S. Congress and legislation being considered by Congress with proposals that are before their state legislatures.

A third purpose stems from the first two—if readers come away with a better understanding of the lawmaking process and the organization of government at the federal, state, and local levels, they may be more inclined to become informed and active participants in decisions that affect their lives and their community.

In an effort to accommodate the diversity found among law making bodies, particularly with regard to state legislatures, we have included extensive appendices and tables that should be an invaluable resource to readers.

Also, throughout the book there may be terms that are in common usage by those familiar with government but that are not part of the everyday vocabulary of the average citizen. To accommodate that discrepancy, we have bold-faced the first occurence of these words in the book and included a glossary of legislative language that can be referred to for help.

Acknowledgments

A project of this nature would not have been possible without the collective expertise of numerous colleagues at the National Conference of State Legislatures (NCSL). Staff of NCSL's Legislative Management Program in

Denver, in particular, were extremely helpful with suggestions. Brenda Erickson, Sally Kittredge, Chris Pattarozzi, Mary Renstrom, Tim Storey, Kae Warnock, and Brian Weberg, the program director, all contributed excellent suggestions for dealing with various segments of the book and could not have been more supportive during the many months of work that went into the writing of this publication. The same can be said for Jon Felde and Melanie Marshall of NCSL's Washington, DC, office. Jon Felde contributed a major portion of the chapter on Congress, including the case study of federal legislation. In the same chapter, Tim Storey wrote the segment on reapportionment.

Finally, a special "thank you" is due Sally Kittredge and Carolyn Alvarez. Without their skill and tireless work, everything else that went into the project would have been to no effect—they were responsible for putting it all together, no simple task.

PART

I

A Case Study

CHAPTER 1

Megan and Friends

Government at all levels affects everything we do every day. We've heard this so often that it probably doesn't register any more. But if we were to take the time to analyze our daily activities, we'd notice that the laws passed by federal, state, and local lawmaking bodies influence the way we live. The case of Megan McNally, a junior at Middle Park High School, for example, illustrates just how broad the scope of this influence is.

Megan is required by the laws in her state to attend school until she is 18, whether she wants to or not. She could drop out, but then she would have her parents to contend with; besides, she wouldn't want to anyway, because she participates in various activities at Middle Park High. She hopes to go on to college after graduation and she can't graduate until she has met the local school board's requirements for a high school diploma. On top of that, Megan will not be accepted at the state university she wants to attend until she meets the requirements of the State Board of Regents—the governing body of the university. Those requirements include a high school diploma.

Megan, who is fortunate to have her own transportation rather than having to ride a bus, picks up her friend, Emily, on her way to school. They are in the middle of an animated conversation when Megan becomes aware of the flashing red light of a patrol car.

"Do you know how fast you were going? Didn't you see that stop sign?" the police officer asks after he pulls them over. "Let me see your driver's license and your car registration."

When it's over, Megan has a ticket for speeding—40 in a 35 mile-per-hour zone and running a stop sign.

What happens at Middle Park High the rest of the day is even more disturbing. Megan plays basketball for the varsity team, which is a prospective contender for the state championship. At a hastily called team meeting her coach informs the squad that there will be no basketball this year, a decision arrived at by the school board during its meeting the previous night.

"The problem is money," her coach explains. "The legislature passed an **appropriations** bill that reduces state funding for most school districts in the state, ours included. What that means is that the school board was forced to cut costs. Girls' basketball is an easy target."

Not being able to play basketball on a team that might have been a state championship contender becomes a minor irritation when Megan learns about the problems of one of her closest friends, Shirley, who confides that life at home is pretty miserable these days. Unlike Megan, Shirley doesn't enjoy the luxury of having her own car—and that's the least of her worries. Shirley's parents are divorced. Her father is supposed to pay child support until Shirley and her younger brother are 18. He is also supposed to help with the expense of their education beyond high school.

"He hasn't come through with a dime in the last four months," Shirley confides, "and it's getting tough at home. I think I've got a job lined up to help out, starting next week. Beyond that, who knows? I don't look past next week anymore."

"Did you say you've got a job lined up?" Jason, a friend of both girls and normally all smiles, was obviously depressed. "I just got fired from mine."

"What's the problem?" Megan asked. "I thought you were the manager's favorite at that pizza place."

"Yeah, right, but I can't do deliveries any more. My driver's license has been suspended."

"What for? What have you been doing?"

"I got nailed for drinking and driving. I only had a few beers. Tested 0.02, but for us minors that's a violation, if you can believe it. New law they passed last year. And besides having my license suspended, I have to put in time at an alcohol and driving education program and then do 40 hours of community service."

Other news making the rounds at Middle Park was a curfew law passed by the city council. Under the new law children 15 and younger must be in by 10 o'clock, and 16- and 17-year-olds must be in by 11 o'clock every night except Friday and Saturday, when they can stay out until midnight. Curfew violators will be fined $56 for the first offense or required to do 15 hours of community service. Repeat offenders face $70 fines, which may be worked off through minimum-wage community service.

"I think the whole thing is unreasonable," Megan said. "The kids who want to go to the late movies are being punished because some other kids misbehaved."

The really big news at school that day, however, was a drug bust. Gossip around the corridors was that the school board set up an undercover drug operation. For about five months two undercover officers posed as transfer students, hoping to observe any illegal activities, especially drug deals. The result was that six students were nabbed for peddling marijuana and three others were accused of selling homemade bombs.

The whole operation, which cost about $50,000 in school district funds, had some students wondering what was going on.

"The first day of class," Rich Jones told Megan and Shirley, "we all knew they were narcs. The one guy was bald. It was pretty obvious that he didn't belong in high school. I thought he was about 30."

What was obvious to Rich, however, was not as obvious to nine other students who were arrested and charged when they attempted to sell marijuana and the homemade bombs.

"Still, spending $50,000 to nail nine people is a lot of money," Rich said. "I think they could have found a better use for that kind of money, like funding girls' basketball."

The activities and the conversations of Megan and her Middle Park friends on the first day of school were influenced and affected by the action of government at the state and local levels.

- Megan got out of bed and went to school for several reasons: (1) her state has a compulsory attendance law, passed by the state legislature; (2) she wants to go to college, and one of the requirements for admission—established by the governing body of the state university—is a high school diploma; (3) to get a high school diploma she must meet requirements established by the local school board.
- Megan got a ticket for exceeding the speed limit, which was set by a law passed by the state legislature. Megan had to show her

driver's license and car registration to the officer who stopped her—both documents were required under laws enacted by the state legislature.

- Girls' basketball was eliminated by the local school board because there was not enough money to fund it. There was not enough money because the state legislature reduced the state appropriation to local school districts.

- Shirley has problems at home because her father has not been making child support payments. There are laws, passed by the state legislature, that require parents to pay child support. There is, in fact, a Bureau of Child Support Enforcement in her state—created by state legislative action—that her mother can go to for help in getting the child support money due from her ex-husband. Shirley may still want to get a job. In that event, her work hours on school days may be restricted under a law passed by the state legislature.

- Jason's problems are of his own making. A law passed by the state legislature suspends driving privileges and requires attendance in an alcohol and driving education program for minors who drink and drive. The same law says that an alcohol concentration of 0.02 constitutes a violation for minors. There are also laws, enacted by the state legislature, that prohibit the sale of liquor to minors, but Jason got around them.

- The newly enacted curfew law was passed by the city council, under authority granted to local governments by the state legislature.

- Finally, the drug bust at Middle Park was an operation the local school board undertook in order to control substance abuse. They decided that was worth $50,000. There are state laws that make drug possession on or near school property a crime.

Here are some other laws, enacted in recent years by various state legislatures, that further illustrate the effect government has on our everyday lives.

- Interest on overdue child support payments accrues at a rate of 10 percent a year. Payments become due after 30 days. Also, child support payments can be extended beyond the age of 18 as long as the child remains in school.

- Legislation enacted by state legislatures provides for reduced tuition at state colleges and universities for members of the National Guard.
- Municipal, county, and regional planning commissions are required to consider the availability of affordable housing in creating master plans for property development.
- Work hours are restricted for students while school is in session, although some exceptions are made. A school superintendent may revoke a student's employment certificate if the student fails four courses in one semester.
- Firearms cannot be sold to minors unless minors are accompanied by a parent. This applies to the private sale of firearms as well as sales by licensed dealers.
- A person suspected of driving under the influence of alcohol (DUI) who refuses to submit to a test to determine the extent of alcohol in the bloodstream will automatically lose his or her driver's license.
- The legislature of a certain state passed an appropriations bill for higher education that significantly reduced funding for state supported universities, colleges, and community colleges. The institutions affected were instructed to increase their tuition rates by at least 15 percent to make up the difference between their **budget** requirements and the amount of state funding.
- After qualifying for welfare subsidies, welfare recipients are allowed 90 days to find a job. Unless it is determined that no jobs are available, welfare payments will be eliminated after 90 days. Exceptions are made for single mothers, who would be allowed one year following the birth of a child before being required to find a job. Single mothers would also be provided vouchers for child care, provided they were working.

These laws, however, are not written in stone. They can be modified by adding or removing clauses, or they can be completely removed from the books. And committed individuals are often the ones who are able to bring these changes about. Megan, if she dedicates herself to it, has a good chance of influencing her state legislature to allocate more money for public schools, thus reinstating girls' basketball. But she must be willing to acquire knowledge about how the system works and then become a participant in the process. This book focuses on how things work in state legislatures, where many of the laws that affect daily life are enacted. For an individual like Megan to make a difference in what happens, it is necessary to understand the legislative process, and how legislators work within it. Most individuals don't even know the names of their state legislators, and that's a good starting point if someone really cares about making a difference. Beyond that, there is much to learn about the workings of state legislatures.

And while the emphasis here is on state legislatures, it also is important to become familiar with the big picture: the roles of local government, the federal government, and the relationship between all three levels of government—state, local, and federal—in order to make a difference. For example, we need to know which level of government is responsible for specific laws and the enforcement of laws, or whether one or more of the governmental levels—local, state, federal—each has a piece of the action. If an individual doesn't know that, they could spend a lot of time spinning their wheels without getting anyplace.

SUMMARY

It is easy to miss the connection between everyday life and governmental action. The case study of Megan and her friends provides examples of the effect laws have on much of what we do, from funding a girls' basketball team to child support payments, jobs, and drivers' licenses.

Getting Started

CHAPTER 2

Making Connections

An understanding of how laws are made is essential for anyone who wants to make a difference, but it is also important to know who makes, executes, and interprets these laws—and where their power comes from. This chapter helps make the connection between the duties and responsibilities of the federal, state, and local levels of government.

L aws that affect everyday life are made at several levels of government, from local school districts and state legislatures to the U.S. Congress in Washington.

Each of those jurisdictions has its place in the whole scheme of government as it is organized in the United States. But to understand the place of state legislatures we need to first understand how our system of government is organized and the relationship between each level of government. In other words, we need to make some connections.

THE THREE BRANCHES OF GOVERNMENT

Government in the United States, whether at the federal, state, or local level is divided into three branches: legislative, executive, and judicial. The reason for this division is to ensure a democratic form of government. Each branch of government has certain responsibilities and powers, providing a system of checks and balances that prevents any one branch from becoming too powerful. The legislative branch has the power to enact laws, which can be **veto**ed by the head of the executive branch—governors in the states, the president in the federal government. The executive branch has the power to carry out programs and provide services but must do so in accordance with laws the legislature has enacted. And the money to operate the executive and judicial branches is appropriated by the legislature. The judicial branch—the courts—checks the power of the legislative branch through its consideration of laws that have been enacted by the legislature. Decisions made by lower courts may be subject to appeal, but if an appeal reaches the nation's highest court, the U.S. Supreme Court, there is no further appeal from the court's decision. At that point, if the law is declared unconstitutional, it is no longer in effect.

The Legislative Branch

This is the branch of government that is the focus of this book. The legislature is the policy-making branch of government. It carries out this responsibility by making laws, which in turn, determine policy. For example, action taken by the legislative branch establishes governmental policy on issues such as abortion: whether abortions are legal; whether state funds may be spent for them; whether teenagers must obtain parental consent for abortions; and other related issues. And whatever policy is determined by the legislative branch must be carried out by the executive branch of government, unless the law is challenged in the courts and is determined to be unconstitutional by the judicial branch. The legislative branch also controls the purse strings of government. It is the legislature that appropriates the money necessary to operate government and to carry out the laws enacted by the legislature.

An important distinction concerning the legislative branch that many people fail to make is the difference between the U.S. Congress and state legislatures. We tend to confuse one with the other. We might, accidentally, refer to state laws and, in the same breath, talk about our representatives in Congress, or we might refer to legislation being considered in Washington, D.C., and confuse it with legislation being considered by our state legislature. We don't make the necessary connections.

Every state has two United States senators—elected members of the United States Senate—which has a total of 100 members. Each state has a certain number of United States representatives—elected members of the United States House of Representatives, which has a total of 435 members from all 50 states. The number of representatives from each state is determined by population. California, the most populous state, for example, has 52 U.S. representatives. Alaska, Delaware, Montana, North Dakota, South Dakota, Vermont, and Wyoming, the least populous states, have one U.S. representative. The U.S. Senate and the U.S. House collectively are referred to as Congress. It is Congress that makes laws that affect the citizens of all 50 states. In every state, U.S. senators are chosen in statewide elections, since they represent the entire state in Congress. In every state except those with only one member of the House, the state's U.S. representatives are elected from separate **districts** determined according to population (districts must be as equal as possible in population).

How about the legislative branch in each state? There are variations from state to state but, generally, the legislative branch consists of a Senate and a House, comparable to the U.S. Congress. Nebraska has a single legislative body, whose members are senators. The number of members in each state legislative body varies, but in every state, members of both the Senate and the House are elected from districts determined by population.

The Executive Branch

In the federal government, the executive branch is headed by the president of the United States. In all 50 states, the executive branch is headed by an elected governor. The executive branch is the arm of government that has the most direct effect on the everyday life of individuals because it is responsible for carrying out—executing—the laws passed by the legislative branch. The executive branch, through the veto power of the president at the federal level and governors at the state level, also acts as a check on the power of the legislative branch. Executive vetoes at both the federal and state levels, however, can be overridden by the legislature, but only by a substantial majority of the members.

The Judicial Branch

This is the system of courts. It is an extremely important factor in a democratic government, although we will not be discussing it at length in this book. The judicial branch is independent of the legislative and executive branches. It acts as a check on the power of the legislative branch by interpreting the laws enacted by the legislative branch. The courts act as a check on the power of the executive branch by having the responsibility to make decisions concerning actions of the executive branch that are challenged by legal action.

The structure of government at the federal and state levels of government—legislative, executive, and judicial—is also found at the local level. A city government, for example, may consist of an elected city council (the legislative branch), an elected mayor (the executive branch), and a judicial branch (municipal courts, e.g., traffic courts). The same pattern is

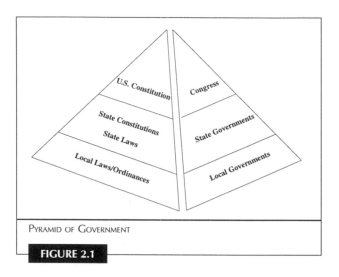

PYRAMID OF GOVERNMENT

FIGURE 2.1

found in county governments: elected county commissioners (the legislative branch), a county manager (not elected, but responsible for the executive branch), and a judicial branch (county courts).

THREE LEVELS OF LAWMAKERS

Of the three branches of government, only the legislative branch *makes* the laws. There are three different levels of lawmakers and each level is responsible for different kinds of laws.

If we use a pyramid as an example of the three levels of lawmakers, at the peak would be Congress—the U.S. House, 435 members; and the Senate, 100 members—state legislatures would be in the middle, and local governments would be at the bottom. Congress[1] is responsible for making laws that affect the nation, all 260 million of us, and all 50 states. The authority for Congress to make laws that affect all the states comes from the U.S. Constitution, a product of the Constitutional Convention of 1787 that was approved in 1788 by the 13 states in existence at the time, and which took effect in 1789. The other 37 states that have become part of the United States since 1789 have done so with the knowledge that the U.S. Constitution is the "supreme law of the land," a phrase that is frequently used. What it means is that the U.S. Constitution, which binds all the states together in our national government, takes precedence over state constitutions and state laws. If there is a conflict between a state constitution

---

[1]For a detailed discussion on the duties of Congress, see Chapter 10.

and the U.S. Constitution, or a state law and a federal law, it is the U.S. Constitution or the federal law that prevails.

Types of Laws Passed by Congress

Here are some examples of issues that are subject to action by Congress because they are matters that affect the citizens of all 50 states:

Federal income taxes. Congress establishes the rates at which earnings are taxed, thus determining the amount that residents of all the states pay to support the federal government and programs that have been authorized by Congress.

Social Security taxes. Employers and individual workers throughout the nation pay taxes into the Social Security fund at rates established by Congress. The Social Security system was passed in the 1930s by Congress to provide monthly benefits to workers when they retire.

Foreign affairs. Our relations with other countries are a matter of national policy, so that is why Congress and the president act for the United States as a whole. Imagine the chaos and uncertainty that could result if individual states had the authority to make agreements with foreign countries. Texas, New Mexico, Arizona, and California all share borders with Mexico, but they are not allowed to make separate agreements of any kind with Mexico. That is a national matter, because whatever agreements may be made affect all 50 states, not just those that happen to be located close to Mexico. The same thing applies to Maine, New Hampshire, Vermont, New York, Michigan, Ohio, Wisconsin, Minnesota, North Dakota, Montana, Idaho, Washington, and Alaska—states that border Canada. None has the authority to make separate agreements with Canada—that's the business of the federal government. And if that were not the way things work, there could be 50 different approaches to how the United States deals with other countries.

National defense. As with foreign affairs, the defense of the country is a national matter over which the individual states have no authority. It's up to Congress to declare war and to provide for the armed forces of the United States (i.e., the Army, Navy, Marines, Air Force, and Coast Guard). In recent history, there has been controversy over whether the president can send U.S. armed forces into action without first getting a declaration of war from Congress. In the Korean conflict (in the 1950s), the president ordered a military action without congressional approval. It was termed a "police action," although it later became a full-scale war. There have been other "police actions" since Korea: Vietnam, Panama, Grenada, Desert Storm, Somalia, and Haiti—all without a declaration of war, or approval for intervention, from Congress.

In 1940, Congress created the Selective Service System to draft men from every state for the armed forces. Since 1973, military service has been on a voluntary basis, but the Selective Service System is still in existence and requires young men to register when they are 18.

There are National Guard units in every state, composed of volunteers. While the Guard can be called out by state governors in cases of emergency within a state, without having to obtain federal approval, the Guard is ultimately under the direction of the president of the United States. The individual state provides facilities and management for the Guard's activities; the federal government provides training and equipment.

Immigration. Congress, rather than individual states, is responsible for making laws that apply to citizens of other countries who may wish to come to the United States to work or, eventually, to become U.S. citizens. This has created problems for states that are neighbors to Mexico, in particular. California and Texas have experienced significant problems with Mexican nationals who find it easy to cross the border into those states, and who then have been provided with services by the state governments of California and Texas, without help from the federal government. Recently, California passed a law which denied these immigrants such services. While controversial, this law exhibits the stress immigrants cause on individual states.

Highways. This is an area where there are shared powers between the state and federal governments. The federal interstate highway system, which criss-crosses the nation, resulted from legislation enacted by Congress. The interstate highways were designed to link all the states (except for Alaska and Hawaii) in a highway system that would be continuous throughout the nation. And since the establishment of the interstate highway system was a creation of Congress, Congress also provided for funding the interstate system by imposing federal taxes on transportation-related items. The money raised by these taxes was apportioned to the states, but the responsibility for actually constructing segments of the highway was left to each state's department of highways or its equivalent.

For a state to receive its share of highway funds, however, Congress imposed some requirements that the states had to meet: for example, establishing a speed limit of 55 miles per hour on interstate highways.

Setting the speed limit on state highways is a responsibility of each state's legislature. In order to be eligible for federal funds to construct the interstate highways, however, state legislatures had to pass legislation establishing the speed limit at 55. This is an example of legislation enacted by Congress that required each of the states, if they wanted to receive federal funds, to pass legislation in order to comply with a law passed by Congress. And since all the states need federal funds for highway construction, state legislatures passed legislation establishing the speed limit at 55, where it remained until recent action by Congress allowed states to set the limit at any speed they choose, without losing their federal funding.

Counterfeiting. The money that you use every day, from one-dollar paper bills to copper pennies, is issued by the United States government. Under the Articles of Confederation, which preceded the Constitution, individual states—and even private institutions such as banks—could issue various denominations of money. This resulted in a chaotic system that varied from state to state. To provide a uniform monetary system—the Constitution reserved to the federal government, not the states, the authority to coin money. And since only the U.S. government has the authority to issue money, it is a federal, not a state, crime to attempt to coin money not issued by the federal government.

Interstate commerce. States have the authority to regulate commerce—that is, trade—that takes place only within an individual state. Thus, state legislatures can pass laws that affect trade within a state's boundaries. Most of the commerce that occurs in the United States today, however, involves trade between more than one state, or interstate commerce. Think, for example, about the clothes we wear every day: shoes, jeans, blouses, T-shirts, socks, or whatever. The odds are that very few of these items were manufactured and sold within a single state. They were probably made in several other states and shipped to your community to be sold by a retailer. That's interstate commerce and it is subject to laws enacted by Congress rather than by a state legislature.

Types of Laws Passed by State Legislatures

In contrast to the duties of the U.S. Congress, the 50 state legislatures make laws that affect only the citizens of their particular state. For example, federal income tax laws, which apply to the residents of all 50 states, are made by Congress. State legislatures may also pass income tax laws, but they apply only to the residents of that one state.

Here are some other examples of responsibilities that come within the jurisdiction of state legislatures.

Education. Public education at every level, from kindergarten through college, is a state responsibility.

That is, the State Legislature:

- Establishes local school districts and determines how much money the state will provide to operate public schools and state colleges and universities.
- Sets the requirements for obtaining a license, or certificate, to teach in the public schools.
- Enacts compulsory attendance laws.
- May require specific subjects to be included in a school's curriculum.
- Determines the minimum number of days in a school year.
- May pass laws restricting work hours on school days.
- May make the possession of drugs or hand guns on or near school property a crime.

The legislature may also prohibit smoking on school property.

Elections. Conducting elections is a state function. Requirements concerning qualifications for office, registration, and voting procedures are subject to laws passed by the state legislature. Here again, however, the federal government has intruded on state responsibilities by requiring certain conditions for federal elections. Most state legislatures, rather than having two separate systems—one for elections of state offices and another for elections of federal offices—have passed legislation to meet the federal requirements, applying them to state as well as federal elections.

Taxation. The division of authority for levying taxes can be a confusing area, because every level of government has some authority to tax in order to raise the money necessary to provide services and to enforce the law.

State legislatures impose taxes to pay for the operation of state government and, in many states, to provide some of the money for public schools and for higher education. Taxes to support state government may come from a variety of sources, including income taxes paid by individuals and businesses, sales taxes, taxes on personal property (a car, for example), inheritance taxes, and taxes on real property (i.e., land, houses, commercial buildings, etc.). State taxes are paid by those who live and/or work in a state.

Units of local government—cities, towns, counties, school districts, and special districts (i.e., recreation or fire districts)—must also have money to operate and provide services for residents. Local governments get money from taxes paid by the citizens who live within the boundaries of a unit of local government. Much of the money needed to operate local governments comes from property and sales taxes. All of these state and local taxes are in addition to federal taxes.

Crime. This is another area that can cause confusion because some crimes are federal offenses and others are state offenses. Most crimes are state offenses, and thus subject to laws enacted by state legislatures. Some crimes, however, involve both state and federal laws. Generally, a crime that involves crossing state lines—for example, kidnapping becomes a federal offense when a person is abducted in one state and taken into another state. Bank robbery is another crime that may involve both state and federal laws.

Highways and traffic regulations. This is still another subject in which there are overlapping responsibilities among federal, state, and local governments. As mentioned above, responsibility for building state highways rests with state governments, subject to laws enacted by the state legislature. Money for interstate highways comes from the federal government, but it is the state legislature that determines where the money will be spent.

Every state requires drivers to be licensed. It is the state legislature that sets the minimum age requirement for getting a driver's license, decides how much the license will cost, and establishes other requirements that must be met in order to get and keep a license.

Every vehicle, from cars to motorcycles to trailer trucks, must be registered. It is the state legislature that sets the registration procedures and the cost of vehicle licenses.

It is also the state legislature that sets speed limits on the highways and determines other rules of the road. To enforce the rules, every state has a state highway patrol, established and funded by the legislature.

Types of Laws Passed by Local Governments

The lowest level of the pyramid of governmental structure is the local level.[2] Don't be misled by the position of local government at the bottom of the pyramid. That has no relationship to its importance to individuals.

---

[2]For a detailed discussion of local government, see Chapter 11.

Local government, in fact, may have a more direct effect on daily life than what goes on in Congress or in state legislature.

There are 83,000 units of local government in the United States. The most common are counties. They are known as parishes in Louisiana and boroughs in Alaska. Only Connecticut and Rhode Island, two of the smaller states, have no county governments. Other units of local government are cities, towns, townships, school districts, and special districts. By whatever name they are identified, these units of local government get their authority to govern from powers granted to them by the state legislature. That is why they occupy a place below the state on our pyramid.

Public Education. In the United States, public education at the elementary and secondary levels has traditionally been a matter of local control. In most states, each school district is governed by a school board—normally composed of elected members. These school boards hire teachers, administrators, and other school district employees. Determining salaries for school district employees also is a function of local school boards, although in some states, salary levels for teachers and administrators are set by the state legislature. Contracts for teachers are a matter between the local board and the teachers in that school district, as well.

School boards also determine how much money will be spent by the district to operate and maintain the schools and the amount of local taxes that will be required to raise the necessary funds. School boards also make decisions about the location, construction, and financing of new schools.

School boards make decisions about the curriculum and about requirements for graduation. Will sex education be offered in a school district, for example? That would ordinarily be a decision for the local school board to make, but in some states sex education or other specific subjects may be mandated by the state legislature.

State supported junior colleges, community colleges, and four-year colleges and universities are usually governed directly by boards or commissions, similar to local school district boards. One difference is that the governing boards of colleges and universities may derive their authority from the state constitution rather than from the legislature, and some boards may be appointed rather than elected.

Other local laws. In addition to education, there are other activities that are regulated by local government.

- **Curfews.** That is the prerogative of local government—in most instances, the city council. The authority to enact curfew and loitering laws, however, is granted to local governments by the state legislature.

- **Law enforcement**. Laws that affect only a particular city or county are made by elected officials in those units of local government and enforced by city police forces and county sheriffs' offices.
- **Housing and commercial developments**. Laws relating to housing developments and commercial developments such as shopping centers and malls are also enacted by units of local government. Proposed housing and commercial developments usually must be approved by a unit of local government, normally elected city or county officials.

SUMMARY

To make the right connections it is necessary to understand the structure of government in the United States. That involves knowing who does what. In this chapter, we have outlined the various levels and branches of government, their authority, their responsibilities, and their relationship to other levels of government.

In the United States, governments—whether they are national, state, or local—are organized around three branches of government: the legislative branch, responsible for determining policy in the laws they enact; the executive branch, which is responsible for implementing the laws enacted by the legislative branch; and the judicial branch, which is responsible for interpreting the laws.

The first level of government is the national government. It consists of Congress, the U. S. Senate and House of Representatives, which is responsible for making national policy by passing laws that apply to all 50 states. Each state has two U.S. senators. The number of representatives from each state is based on population, and range from 52 in California to one in Alaska, Delaware, Montana, North Dakota, South Dakota, Vermont, and Wyoming. The executive branch, headed by the president, is responsible for carrying out laws passed by the legislative branch; and the judicial branch is responsible for interpreting laws passed by the legislative branch. The authority for all three branches of the federal government comes from the U.S. Constitution, which takes precedence over state constitutions.

The second level of government is state government. It operates in a manner similar to the national government. The difference is that state actions apply only to that state, no others. In every state except Nebraska, the legislative branch consists of two **chambers**, a Senate and a House. The number of senators and house members varies from state to state. The executive branch, headed by the governor, is responsible for carrying out the laws for that state, and the judicial branch is responsible for interpreting state laws. Authority for the actions of all three branches of government comes from the state constitution.

The third level is local government. Although there are many variations, local government is structured similarly to federal and state governments. In particular, one often finds a division between the legislative and executive branches in city and county governments. The major difference is that most local governmental units get their authority from laws enacted by the state legislature, although some jurisdictions derive their authority from the state constitution. For example, charters that give specific powers to cities in various areas of governing may be included in a state's constitution.

CHAPTER

•••••••••

The Role of Staff

The role of staff in the legislative process is essential, although it is hardly ever witnessed by the public. Staff does not have a vote in the lawmaking process but may significantly affect the chances of the success or failure of legislation, as we shall see in this chapter.

M embers of a state legislature, members of Congress, and members of local government are elected to represent their **constituents**. They consider proposed legislation. They vote on legislation. They are accountable, through the election process, for their actions. What is frequently overlooked, however, is the role played by staff in the lawmaking process. That may be because staff are not elected to their positions, do not vote on legislation, and aren't accountable to constituents for their actions.

An understanding of how laws are made, however, requires an understanding of the role of staff, whether at the federal, state, or local level of government. The focus of this chapter will be on the role of staff in state legislatures, although the discussion will be relevant to lawmaking at the federal and local levels as well. The difference in staff at the three levels of government is primarily one of numbers: the U.S. Congress has 535 elected members in the House and Senate and an estimated 23,000 staff. That is an average of 47 to 56 staff persons for each of the 535 members of Congress. The total number of staff in all 50 state legislatures is estimated at 33,000 for 7,424 state legislators, an average of slightly more than 4 staff persons for each legislator. New York has the highest total—approximately 4,000 staff for 211 members of the House and Senate, an average of 19 staff for each member. As might be expected, elected officials at the local level have the fewest number of staff for each official.

What matters more than numbers, however, is the role that staff play in the lawmaking process. The importance of staff at all levels of the legislative process is recognized by those who are familiar with the way legislative bodies operate. Ultimately, decisions are made by elected officials, but those decisions may be heavily influenced by the input of staff.

The complexity and the numbers of public problems that legislators must consider have multiplied year by year. In today's world it is impossible for members of a state legislature to do the research necessary to provide the information needed to make informed decisions on all the public policy questions confronting them. Even in smaller states, there are multi-billion dollar appropriations **bills** that require votes by legislators. And there are hundreds of bills introduced at legislative sessions on every conceivable subject, from public schools to crime. That makes it necessary for legislators to depend on staff to gather the information needed to make decisions on public policy. State legislatures have moved away from dependence on external sources for information in favor of in-house staff resources. That has meant an increase in the number of staff. In its policy-making role, the legislative branch at the state level has also become increasingly independent from the executive branch, and that, too, has led to an increase in the number and the importance of staff in every state.

Over the last 25 years, state legislatures have become more professional in their operations, including significant changes in staffing patterns. And while no two state legislatures operate in precisely the same manner, there are similarities in the way all legislative staff operations are structured.

TYPES OF LEGISLATIVE STAFF

There are six types of legislative staffs. In some states, all six can be found; in others, there is a combination of various staffing patterns.

1. During legislative sessions, there are a myriad of details that must be taken care of in order for the legislature to operate effectively. The chief legislative staff officer—whether it is the secretary of the Senate, the clerk of the House, or a designated legislative staff director—is responsible for staff support of bills under consideration by the full membership—from introduction and **reading** of bills, to preparation of **calendar**s, tracking **amendments** offered during **debate**, recording votes, the publication of

journals that reflect **floor** action, posting committee **hearing** schedules, and **engrossing** and **enrolling** bills. In most legislatures these are full-time positions, augmented by additional staff during legislative sessions.

Knowing where to go for information is necessary for anyone who wishes to follow the activities of a legislature during a session. Where is a specific bill in the legislative process (that is, what is its **status**)? What committee hearings are scheduled, and when and where will they be held? What bills are on the calendar of the House or Senate for consideration? Where can I get a copy of the journal for the House or Senate? A copy of a bill? This is the type of information that is available from the office of the secretary of the Senate, the clerk of the House, or the designated staff director of either legislative chamber.

2. Research on specific legislation that may be considered by the legislature is frequently the responsibility of a separate, nonpartisan, full-time professional staff. They provide background information on bills that have been introduced or that may be under consideration for **introduction** and respond to the requests of members for information on specific subjects. In many states, they staff the various committees of the legislature, which may involve recording of committee votes and preparation of minutes, amendments, and committee reports.

Research staff are identified by a variety of names: **Legislative Council**, Legislative Services, Legislative Reference Bureau, Legislative Commission, and others. In some states a single research staff serves both houses of the legislature; in others there are separate staffs for the House and Senate. In any event, research staff are a major resource for legislators and play an important role in the legislative process.

Most states also have a legislative library that specializes in policy research and is located close to legislative offices as either a part of the legislative research agency or of something that works closely with it. Library staff focus on legislative priorities and provide professional services such as maintaining reference and public policy periodical collections and performing online searches for information. Like other aspects of state legislatures, these libraries range greatly in number of staff, size of collection and budget, and level of professionalization. In states where there is no legislative library there is generally a division within the state library that handles legislative needs.

3. Bill drafting, a major function that requires technical legal expertise, often is the responsibility of a separate staff of attorneys—an Office of Legislative Legal Services, for example. Legal staff draft bills requested by members and by legislative committees.

There is no universal requirement that bills must be drafted by legislative staff. Technically, bills can be drafted by anyone, but most legislatures require that bills written by outsiders must be reviewed by the legislative legal staff to be sure that they conform to the legislature's bill format. Legal staff also draft amendments to proposed legislation, and may also have responsibility for the revision and publication of a state's **statutes**, laws that are enacted in each legislative **session**.

4. The appropriation of money to operate state government and the levying of taxes to produce the necessary revenue are the prerogative of the legislature. The appropriation process varies from state to state, but in a number of states the legislative budgeting process is the responsibility of a full-time staff of fiscal analysts who look at the funding requests of state executive branch agencies and make recommendations to the legislature about how much money is expected to be available and how much should be appropriated to individual state agencies. The fiscal staff also makes recommendations on spending for other purposes such as state appropriations for public schools and state supported colleges and universities. In some states, the budget staff is within the legislature's House and Senate appropriations committees; in a few states there is a **joint** budget **committee** with members from both chambers.

5. A number of states have separate partisan staffs for the Republican and Democratic **caucuses** of both chambers. They provide research aimed at developing party positions and legislation on issues before the legislature.

6. In larger states with full-time legislatures, members may be provided with one or more personal staff for their offices at the capitol and, at times, with staff for offices in their legislative districts. Part of a legislator's job involves responding to requests of the people they represent. In populous districts such as those in California, where a member may represent 750,000 people, district offices and full-time personal staff enable legislators to provide services to their constituents.

SUMMARY

Legislators make the final decisions on legislation, whether it is about proposals they may sponsor, amendments to bills, appropriations for state programs and services, or how they may vote on matters that come before the legislature. And while legislative staff have no vote, they play an important role in the process. In every legislature, it is the responsibility of staff to do research, to draft bills and amendments, and to be responsible for the efficient operation of the legislature during sessions. In some states, partisan and personal staff also contribute to the process by conducting specialized research on partisan issues and by responding to the requests of constituents.

CHAPTER

The Role of Lobbyists

lobby—To seek to influence legislators to pass (legislation).

lobbyist—One employed to influence legislators to introduce or vote for **measures** *favorable to the interest....represented.*

—The American Heritage Dictionary

A nother major factor in the legislative process is the role of lobby ists. Lobbying occurs at every stage of the process, from ideas for legislation, to drafting, introduction, committee consideration, floor consideration and votes on final passage, conference committees, and the governor's action. In this chapter we will take a look at what lobbying is and how it influences the success or failure of legislation.

Lobbyists are major players in the game of legislation, so much so that the lobbying corps in state capitols is frequently referred to as "The Third House." Lobbyists are in the same category as legislative staff when it comes to making decisions about whether a bill will be introduced, and in voting on a proposal—making final decisions about voting is something that only members of the legislature, elected to represent the people of their district and their state, can do. Like legislative staff, however, lobbyists may have considerable influence in the lawmaking process. Hired to represent the interests of a group, a business firm, or even an individual, in some instances, during sessions of the legislature, lobbyists follow legislation that might affect the special interests of their clients and seek to influence its passage or defeat.

Lobbyists have been part of the state legislative scene since at least the early 1800s when the term was used to describe individuals who frequented the lobbies of the legislative chambers in New York's state capitol, seeking to influence the passage or defeat of bills under consideration. The first reference was to "lobby-agents," which was later simplified to "lobbyists."

The business of lobbying has grown significantly since those early times in New York. The lobbying corps in the 50 state capitols now numbers around 42,000—almost six lobbyists to every state legislator.

In earlier times it may have been possible for legislators to become familiar with the details of most of the proposals they were called upon to consider. Now, however, it is unrealistic to expect a legislator to become an expert on every subject that comes before the legislature, including the details of multi-billion dollar budgets that are common to most of the states. The most effective legislators are those who concentrate on becoming experts in one or two subject areas. On legislation outside their area of expertise they rely on other members whose knowledge and judgment they respect, on legislative staff, and on non-members with expertise—including lobbyists.

In our representative form of government the average citizen has neither the time nor the knowledge of how legislatures operate to be actively involved in the lawmaking process. Acting collectively, however, individuals can influence the course of public policy decisions. Enter the lobbyist, who works for such a group or company wishing to influence legislation.

There are two major categories of lobbying. First, a lobbyist may work for one or more entities: a telephone company, an airline, a chemical company, a trucking firm. Second, a lobbyist also may work for an association or a similar organization whose members have common legislative objectives but who may live in communities throughout a state. In either case, a lobbyist tracks legislation that may affect a client, provides information to legislators, and works to enact or defeat legislation that would affect a client.

Despite the public's negative perception of lobbying, it is—or can be—an honorable endeavor. There are examples, however, when that has not been the case (i.e., lobbyists have bought the votes of legislators willing to sell their vote for a price). Scandals involving bribery have occurred in several states—examples include Arizona, Kentucky, New Mexico, and South Carolina—which leads to the perception that all 42,000 lobbyists are dishonorable, a perception that obviously isn't true.

In going about their work in an honorable fashion, lobbyists have certain obligations. These are best expressed in a Florida Senate rule which says that:

> A lobbyist shall supply facts, information and opinions of principals to legislators from the point of view from which he openly declares. A lobbyist shall not offer or propose anything to improperly influence the official act, decision or vote of a legislator.
>
> A lobbyist, by personal example...shall uphold the honor of the legislative process by the integrity of his relationship with legislators.
>
> A lobbyist shall not knowingly and willfully falsify a material fact or make any false, fictitious, or fraudulent statement or representation or make or use any writing or document knowing the same contains any false, fictitious, or fraudulent statements or entry.

Lobbyists who operate under those principles have become a part of the legislative process, serving a useful purpose.

The best lobbyists are those who bring to their work an appreciation of the not-so-obvious factors of how legislative bodies work: the personalities of individual legislators, the importance of timing, and a willingness to compromise. Compromise is at the heart of the legislative process. Legislation is rarely passed without change from the form in which it was introduced. The purpose of hearings, committee deliberations, and floor debate is to provide an opportunity for different views to be considered and to reach general agreement on questions of public policy. Reaching general agreement nearly always requires some compromise along the way.

Being aware of these factors, the work of successful lobbyists may begin well in advance of a legislative session—getting sponsors for proposed legislation, developing testimony to be presented at committee hearings, perhaps arranging for members of an association to testify at hearings, and discussing compromises that may be necessary to get a bill passed. There is no single method that guarantees success for a lobbyist. The most essential ingredient for long term success, however, is integrity.

Besides providing information to legislators, lobbyists also seek to establish a reputation among legislative staff as being a competent, accurate source of timely information. Experienced lobbyists recognize the significant role of staff at all stages of the legislative process, and, therefore, look to provide them with useful statistics and with information concerning the effect of proposed legislation.

All the states have laws governing the activities of lobbyists. In many states there are restrictions on gifts, campaign contributions, and the specific dollar amounts that lobbyists are allowed to spend on legislators for such things as meals and entertainment. Several states are so restrictive that a cup of coffee or two is about as much as a lobbyist is allowed to spend on a legislator in a day's time.

Each state requires lobbyists to register. In every state except Wyoming and Montana, registered lobbyists must file periodic reports, primarily about income—what they have spent on their lobbying activities and, in some states, the names of legislators they have entertained or on whom they have expended more than a specific amount of money. In Mississippi, for example, lobbyists must report the names of legislators on whom they have spent more than $10 for meals, coffee, or anything else.

It should also be noted that there are no basic differences in lobbying at the federal, state, and local levels. There is a difference in the number of lobbyists, of course, with more at the federal level than in an individual state, and more at state legislatures than at the local level, but their goal, at any level, is to work for the passage or defeat of legislation that would affect their clients. Also, it is not unusual to find lobbyists who work for clients at all three levels of governments.

SUMMARY

Lobbyists are major players in the legislative game; they follow legislation for clients who hire the lobbyists for their knowledge of how the legislature works. In simpler times it was possible for most citizens to take a direct part in making decisions about the laws, but that is no longer possible. This is where lobbyists come into the picture. They are employed by groups of people with similar interests to track or influence the success or failure of legislative proposals that affect the interests of the group.

To be effective, lobbyists must be thoroughly familiar with the legislative process, including the role of the legislature's staff, and must provide information to both legislators and staff. In addition, lobbyists are required to abide by the laws governing their activities.

CHAPTER 5

The Beginning of a Bill: From Idea to the Hopper

In this chapter we will discuss where ideas for laws come from and how they get introduced to the legislature as bills. In addition, we will meet eight individuals whose proposals for laws we will follow through the lawmaking process.

THE MECHANICS OF LAWMAKING

The basics of the lawmaking process are simple. A bill is introduced. A committee considers the bill and either rejects it or sends it to the legislative **chamber**—the House or Senate—to be passed or rejected by a vote of all the members. It then goes through the same procedure in the second chamber. When both houses have agreed upon the same wording, the bill goes to the governor. If the governor signs it, it becomes law. But the governor can also **veto** the bill. If the governor vetoes it, the legislature has an opportunity to pass the bill over the governor's objections, and it becomes law without the governor's signature. In some states the bill can become law if the governor takes no action within a specified number of days.

There are variations in that procedure among the states but that is the basic process. Nebraska is an exception because it only has one legislative chamber rather than two.

But that's not all there is to it. We've left out the most important ingredient the people involved. The legislative process, on paper, is a mechanical process. There are many variations from state to state but it's basically the same in all states as well as in the U.S. Congress. What makes it different from a machine is the interaction of the legislators, and their personalities, who were elected to make the laws for your state.

State legislative bodies come in various sizes, from New Hampshire's 400-member House to Alaska's 20-member Senate. And in any organization of 20 or more individuals there is likely to be an inner circle: the power structure. That's especially true in legislatures. Every member of a legislative body has one vote. The votes of some members, however, carry more weight than others because they are part of the inner circle, the power structure, and the decisions they make affect what happens to proposed legislation.

CATEGORIES OF STATE LEGISLATURES

Category 1 — Full-time, large staff, relatively high pay, stable membership:

California	New York
Illinois	Ohio
Massachusetts	Pennsylvania
Michigan	Wisconsin
New Jersey	

Category 2 — In-between, hybrid:

Alabama	Minnesota
Alaska	Mississippi
Arizona	Missouri
Colorado	Nebraska
Connecticut	North Carolina
Delaware	Oklahoma
Florida	Oregon
Hawaii	South Carolina
Iowa	Tennessee
Kansas	Texas
Kentucky	Virginia
Louisiana	Washington
Maryland	

Category 3 — Part-time, low pay, small staff, high turnover:

Arkansas	New Mexico
Georgia	North Dakota
Idaho	Rhode Island
Indiana	South Dakota

Category 3 — Part-time, low pay, small staff, high turnover: (continued)

Maine	Utah
Montana	Vermont
Nevada	West Virginia
New Hampshire	Wyoming

Courtesy of Karl Kurtz, National Conference of State Legislatures

For example, the **Speaker** of the House and the **President** of the Senate are powerful positions. They are the major leadership positions, elected by the legislative members of the **majority party**. In many legislatures, they have the final say about who will serve on each committee. They may also appoint the chair and vice chair of each committee. The Speaker and the Senate President may also assign bills to the various committees and set the calendar, or **agenda**, for each session. When votes are taken, they have only one vote, but their power, outlined above, has much to do with whether a bill ever gets to the floor of the chamber for a vote. If the Speaker and the President of the Senate support a bill, it usually has an excellent chance of being passed. If they are strongly opposed to a bill, it may never see the light of day.

Two other examples of a legislature's inner circle are the **majority leader** and the committee chairs. In some state legislatures the floor leader and committee chairs are elected by the members of their political party; in others, they are appointed by the Speaker. In either case, they exercise influence beyond their individual vote. The majority floor leader works closely with the Speaker of the House or the President of the Senate in scheduling bills for consideration by the full membership and controls debate when bills reach the floor. Committee chairs control the flow of legislation that is assigned to their committee. In some states, committee chairs have the power to determine whether bills will be considered by their committee; in others, every bill assigned to a committee must be brought up for a vote, thus diminishing the power of the chair.

But even with committee chairs it depends on the committee; some committees are more powerful than others. The "money" committees—finance, budget, or appropriations—are the most influential in the state legislative process because they have the final say in recommending taxes to produce revenue and appropriations to spend that revenue on state programs.

Up to this point we've discussed only majority party members who may be part of the inner circle. In every legislature there are members of the **minority party** who also are part of the power structure, although to a lesser extent. The minority floor leader, as the leader of the minority party, can be expected to have at least some influence on decisions that members of the minority party make on legislation. And during any legislative session there are likely to be occasions when a few votes—sometimes, even one vote—from the minority can be the difference between passage or defeat of legislation. The **minority leader**'s place in the power structure may also depend on the number of members from the two major political parties in the legislature. If one party has a significant margin—say 122 Democrats to 35 Republicans in the House and 31 Democrats to nine Republicans in the Senate, which were the actual numbers for Massachusetts in a recent session—the minority leader may be left out in the cold, because the majority party has a comfortable margin of votes on any question and can afford to ignore the minority.

If the partisan makeup of the legislature is much closer, however—say 19 Republicans to 16 Democrats in the Senate and 34 Republicans to 31 Democrats in the House, which were the actual numbers for Colorado in a recent session—the minority leader's support becomes essential. In those instances, where only a few votes separate the majority from the minority, the minority leader cannot be ignored by the majority leaders. He or she must be counted among that legislature's power structure for at least as long as the division between the two major parties remains close.

In some years there have been examples of an unprecedented sharing of power, made necessary by a tie between the members of the two parties. The Florida Senate, for example, had a 20-20 division between Democratic and Republican members, and the Michigan and Nevada House chambers had a similar division between the two major parties. In each case, the leadership—President of the Senate in Florida and Speaker of the House in Michigan and Nevada—became a shared arrangement between the two major parties. That seldom happens, however. One party normally has a majority of the seats in each legislative chamber, enabling it to elect the leadership.

And in any legislative body there will be some members who are part of the power structure even though they hold none of the leadership positions. They are usually found among the inner circle for intangible reasons: they may be highly respected for their knowledge, for their experience, or they may simply have personalities that fit well with any group. They will most often be found working quietly behind the scenes. They are not the speechmakers, but when they have something to say, people listen.

THERE OUGHT TO BE A LAW!

How often have we heard this? "There ought to be a law keeping kids off the streets at night!" Or, "There ought to be a law against graffiti!" Or, "There ought to be a law ...." about almost anything that is a concern of the moment or that may have been the subject of public discussion for some time.

Where do ideas for laws originate? They come from several primary sources: elected officials, professional associations (doctors, lawyers, teachers, dentists, nurses, optometrists, chiropractors), special interest groups (realtors, bankers, merchants, plumbers, electricians, chambers of commerce), government agencies, individual citizens, and civic groups.

The campaigns of elected officials may focus on issues they seek to translate into legislation when they take office. Government agencies may propose legislation they believe to be necessary to the operation of their agencies. Professional and trade associations may seek legislation they perceive as a benefit to their members. Special interest groups may champion proposals to achieve their goals. Individual citizens play a role when they become concerned enough about a specific problem to request that their legislators introduce legislation to do something about it.

Eight Examples

1. Margaret Justice had never been active in politics until she became concerned about the easy availability of handguns. She was shocked when her two teenagers came home from their suburban high school one afternoon talking about students who were bringing handguns to school.

   When she discovered that getting handguns was relatively easy for high school students, she thought there should be a law banning handgun sales to minors so she decided to run for the state House of Representatives. During the campaign she pledged to introduce such legislation. She won the election and was sworn in as a member of the majority party in the House.

2. Lyle Spahnser is in his second term as a representative from the state's largest city, which has a metropolitan population of 3 million. An attorney whose district includes several areas where gangs are active, Representative Spahnser decided to address the problem of

gangs by introducing legislation designed to prevent juvenile and gang-related crimes. He was urged to do so by several parents in his district and by a group of realtors concerned about a decline in real estate prices resulting from the activity of gangs.

3. Brian Caucus is a veteran legislator. He served three terms in the House before being elected to the Senate, where he is in his second term. A retired teacher, he represents a rural area of the state that includes several small to medium sized towns located in five counties. Senator Caucus has been approached by parents in his district who say that, even in their small towns and counties, curfews are needed to control the late-night activities of juveniles.

4. Vito Martinez was elected governor on the strength of his campaign pledge to reduce the cost of state government. To carry out that pledge, his budget proposal to the legislature recommended a reduction in the state appropriation for public schools. Governor Martinez has also gone on record as favoring legislation to reduce crime, but he does not favor gun control legislation. The governor, of course, does not have a vote in the legislature but he does have the power to sign or veto laws passed by the legislature.

5. James DeMoulin has tried for several years to persuade the legislature to pass a law requiring motorcyclists to wear helmets. As director of the state Department of Highways he is concerned that his agency will lose $5 million in federal funds if no helmet law is enacted. A law passed by the U.S. Congress provides for the withholding of federal funds from states that do not have a mandatory helmet law for motorcycle riders.

6. Frank Thorne is a professional lobbyist. He lobbies for several associations, working with legislators to pass or defeat legislation endorsed or opposed by the groups that employ him. One of his clients is the National Rifle Association, a group that opposes gun control.

7. Megan McNally and friends are the Middle Park High School students introduced in the introductory case study. Megan and friends are upset because the legislature reduced state funding for public schools. They have decided to lobby their senator and representatives to support a **supplemental appropriation** that would increase state support of public schools for kindergarten through high school.

8. Kae Kittredge is a private citizen who feels strongly about the need for legislation to tighten the state's domestic violence laws. Her interest stems from the problems of a close friend who has suffered repeated physical abuse but who has not been able to get adequate

protection because of the state's lenient domestic violence laws. Mrs. Kittredge would like to see the legislature enact laws requiring time in jail for offenders and stricter enforcement of restraining orders.

IN THE HOPPER

There is a prescribed order of events that must occur in order for an idea to become a law (see Table 1). Wherever the idea originates, it must first be drafted and introduced as a bill before it can be considered further.

Rules

A bill is a proposal. It does not become a law until passed by the legislature and signed by the governor. Every legislature has **rules** that govern the introduction of bills. The rules vary from state to state, but there are some requirements that are common to all states.

Only a member of the legislature can introduce a bill. If Governor Vito Martinez wants the legislature to consider a bill on crime or an appropriation for public schools, he must get a member of the legislature to introduce it. Also, James DeMoulin, director of the state Department of Highways, may be adamant about the need for a helmet law, but he's out of luck unless he can convince a legislator to introduce a bill on the subject.

Bills must comply with the legislature's format for bills. In theory, bills may be written by anyone. That seldom happens, but no state prohibits an individual citizen or a group from putting their ideas into writing as a proposed bill. Those drafted by individuals or groups outside the legislature, however, are reviewed by the legislature's staff attorneys to be sure they conform to that state's format for bills. Kae Kittredge may feel strongly enough about domestic violence laws to write a bill she wants her legislator to introduce, but whatever she comes up with will have to be submitted to the legislature's staff attorneys for compliance with the format for bills.

Besides those two basic requirements, there are others that apply in some states—but not all.

Deadlines. To speed up the process and to reduce the logjam that frequently occurs at the end of a legislative session, all states except Minnesota, Ohio, Pennsylvania, Rhode Island, and Wisconsin have adopted deadlines for introducing bills. In the states that have deadlines, however, there are a number of variations. In Alabama, Idaho, Michigan, New Jersey, South Carolina, and Washington there are deadlines for the intro-

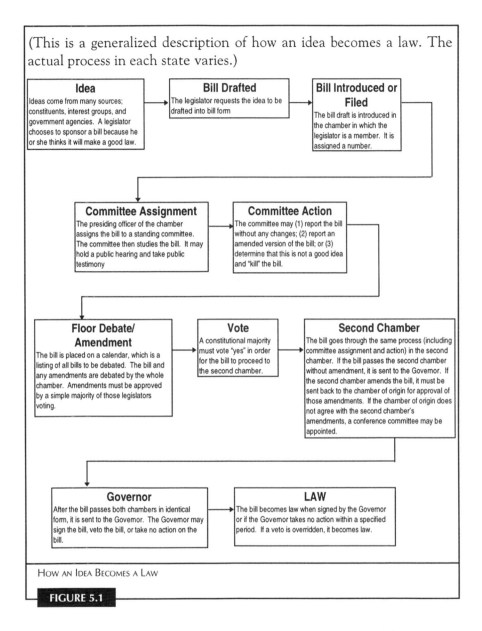

(This is a generalized description of how an idea becomes a law. The actual process in each state varies.)

Idea
Ideas come from many sources; constituents, interest groups, and government agencies. A legislator chooses to sponsor a bill because he or she thinks it will make a good law.

Bill Drafted
The legislator requests the idea to be drafted into bill form

Bill Introduced or Filed
The bill draft is introduced in the chamber in which the legislator is a member. It is assigned a number.

Committee Assignment
The presiding officer of the chamber assigns the bill to a standing committee. The committee then studies the bill. It may hold a public hearing and take public testimony

Committee Action
The committee may (1) report the bill without any changes; (2) report an amended version of the bill; or (3) determine that this is not a good idea and "kill" the bill.

Floor Debate/ Amendment
The bill is placed on a calendar, which is a listing of all bills to be debated. The bill and any amendments are debated by the whole chamber. Amendments must be approved by a simple majority of those legislators voting.

Vote
A constitutional majority must vote "yes" in order for the bill to proceed to the second chamber.

Second Chamber
The bill goes through the same process (including committee assignment and action) in the second chamber. If the bill passes the second chamber without amendment, it is sent to the Governor. If the second chamber amends the bill, it must be sent back to the chamber of origin for approval of those amendments. If the chamber of origin does not agree with the second chamber's amendments, a conference committee may be appointed.

Governor
After the bill passes both chambers in identical form, it is sent to the Governor. The Governor may sign the bill, veto the bill, or take no action on the bill.

LAW
The bill becomes law when signed by the Governor or if the Governor takes no action within a specified period. If a veto is overridden, it becomes law.

HOW AN IDEA BECOMES A LAW

FIGURE 5.1

duction of bills in the Senate, but none in the House. In California there are deadlines for bill introductions in the House, but none in the Senate. In the Delaware House, deadlines apply only during the second year of each two-year legislative session. In Nevada, deadlines apply to legislation requested by state or local government agencies, but not to legislators.

Restrictions on the number of bills that may be introduced. Until she won her campaign for election to the legislature, Representative Justice was not aware that there were restrictions on the number of bills a member could introduce in a legislative session. Her state is one of ten with these limits. In her state the limit is six in each regular session. Because of that, Representative Justice will have to pick and choose the bills she proposes. But since her campaign focused on prohibiting handgun sales to minors, she has no problem deciding to make that subject the first of the six she's allowed.

Prefiling. In most states, bills can be introduced officially only when the House or Senate is in session. To streamline the process, however, all but five states allow—but do not require—legislators to **prefile** bills before the beginning of a session (i.e., Georgia, Idaho, Michigan, Rhode Island, and Wisconsin). When the draft of a bill has been completed, the sponsor may prefile it with the Clerk of the House or the Secretary of the Senate and it will then be ready to be officially introduced on the first day of the session. Prefiling speeds up the legislative process by making it possible for the legislature's House or Senate staff to complete the paper work that must be done before a bill can be "tossed in the **hopper**"—that is, officially introduced while the House or Senate is in session. If prefiling were not available, there could be as many as 100 or 200 bills waiting to go through the necessary paper work before any of them could be introduced on the first day of a legislative session. With prefiling, a large number of bills are ready for introduction immediately and committee work on bills can begin the first or second day of a session.

Drafting Legislation

Before proposed legislation is ready for introduction it must be drafted. That's another term for "written." Drafting a bill, however, is more than a simple writing task. Most bills are written by legal specialists on the legislature's staff—i.e., attorneys experienced in drafting bills, knowledgeable about the required form, and aware of existing laws or constitutional provisions that may be affected by, or conflict with, the proposed legislation. Legislative lawyers who draft bills do so at the request of legislators. During a session, the legislature's lawyers may be asked to draft several thousand bills dealing with a wide variety of subjects. The statistics for the following states are from the 1991 legislative sessions.

Arkansas. There were 2,000 bills introduced during the legislative session. Most were drafted by legislative staff lawyers.

Georgia. The legislature had 5,000 requests for bill drafts. Except for 30 appropriations bills, all 5,000 were drafted by legislative lawyers.

Idaho. Even in a less populous state like Idaho, there were 1,126 requests for new legislation. Only a handful of those did not originate in Idaho's Legislative Council.

Indiana. In the 1991 regular session there were 1,955 requests. Of these, 1,042 were eventually introduced in the House and 631 in the Senate. All bills were drafted by Indiana's Legislative Services Agency.

North Carolina. There were 2,221 requests. The legislative legal staff also drafts 100 to 200 bills each session for committees and **interim** study committees.

South Carolina. The legislature's legal staff had requests for 4,412 bills. Of those requested, 2,041 were introduced and most of those were drafted by the legislature's lawyers.

Texas. There were 10,000 requests for bill drafts, plus another 1,593 for resolutions and **memorials**—which are much simpler than bills and, if passed, do not carry the force of law.

Washington. Requests for bill drafts totaled 6,973, of which 2,522 were introduced. About half of the bills introduced are written from scratch by legislative bill drafters.

Wisconsin. The Legal Section of the Legislative Reference Bureau had 6,184 requests for bills and resolutions, and drafted 5,043. Of these, 1,992 were introduced.

Besides responding to requests for bills on specific subjects, it is the legislature's lawyers who review bills written by persons outside the legislature, to be sure that what has been drafted is in the proper format.

A Bill Concerning the Sale of Firearms

After her victory in November, newly elected Representative Margaret Justice realized that, with no experience as a legislator, she would not be able to draft legislation on her own. She went to the Office of Legislative Legal Services a few weeks after the election.

"Look," she said to the legislative staff lawyer, "one of my campaign issues was gun control. I promised to sponsor legislation banning the sale of handguns to minors. I may be new to all this, but I have sense enough to realize that I don't know the first thing about the technical requirements of writing a bill. So I want a bill drafted to accomplish what I promised during the campaign."

"To do that," the attorney advised her, "we will have to **amend** the current statutes to add a new **section**. And that raises several questions. What age are you talking about? And do you want to include a ban on the sale of other firearms such as rifles and shotguns?"

After further discussion, Representative Justice and the legislative attorney agreed on the specifics of her bill. It would prohibit the sale of any firearm, except for rifles and shotguns, to anyone under 21. It would prohibit the sale of any firearm, including rifles and shotguns, to anyone under 18.

"I'll give you the draft when I have it finished, probably in two or three weeks," the legislative lawyer told Representative Justice. "You may want to consider prefiling it in order to get it moving through the process early."

A Bill to Prevent Juvenile and Gang-Related Crimes

Representative Lyle Spahnser, an attorney in his second term in the House, developed his own version of a bill to prevent juvenile and gang-related crimes. His draft included a statute creating a new offense: "the active participation in a criminal street gang," and provided penalties for "any person who actively participates in any criminal street gang with knowledge that the members of such criminal street gang engage in...a pattern of criminal gang activity." Representative Spahnser's bill included definitions of "criminal street gang" and "pattern of criminal gang activity." Representative Spahnser's bill also made parents or legal guardians responsible for the participation of a juvenile under their control in a "pattern of criminal gang activity." His draft was checked by the Office of Legislative Legal Services for format and its affect on existing law. The legislative attorney assigned to review Representative Spahnser's bill suggested several changes needed to conform with the legislature's bill format and amendments to existing statutes.

A Bill Relating to Curfews, Loitering, and Graffiti

Senator Brian Caucus, the most experienced of the three legislators, preferred to leave to the Office of Legislative Legal Services the drafting of his bill which authorizes counties to adopt ordinances discouraging loitering and graffiti by juveniles, as well as imposing curfews.

"This is an area that I know will require careful drafting," he told the legislative attorney working with him, "so I want to leave the whole job of writing the bill up to you. What I want to do is introduce legislation that will authorize counties to impose curfews, as well as penalties on juveniles for loitering and graffiti."

An Appropriation for Public Schools

Vito Martinez conducted a vigorous campaign that included a proposal for the reduction in state funding of public schools. After his election, however, he had been besieged with requests to increase the state's support of public schools. As a result, he changed his mind and decided to request a **supplemental appropriation** for state funding. He instructed his staff attorney to draft a supplemental appropriation to increase the state's funding of public schools by $25 million. As with all bills, the governor's attorney gave this draft to the legislature's attorneys for review. And, later, when the governor's request for a supplemental appropriation is introduced, of course, it must be sponsored by a member of the legislature. Governor Martinez asked Senator Brian Caucus, who chairs the Senate Appropriations committee, to carry the bill. Senator Caucus agreed to be the sponsor.

A Bill Requiring Motorcyclists to Wear Helmets

James DeMoulin, with the approval of the governor, asked the attorney for his department to draft legislation requiring helmets for motorcycle riders. As with Governor Martinez's supplemental appropriation for schools, DeMoulin had to find a legislator willing to carry the helmet bill. He discussed the legislation with Representative Lyle Spahnser, a member of the House Transportation committee, and he agreed to be the sponsor.

A Bill Concerning Domestic Violence

Kae Kittredge wrote a bill requiring police who respond to calls involving domestic violence to arrest alleged spouse abusers, even though the spouse refused to sign a complaint. Her bill also required the alleged abuser to spend some time in jail. She also included tighter enforcement of restraining orders issued by the courts.

When she completed her draft she called her newly elected representative for whom she had campaigned, Margaret Justice.

"Margaret, I feel strongly that something needs to be done to strengthen the domestic violence laws and I've written a bill designed to do that. Will you consider sponsoring it?"

"Kae, I can only introduce six bills this session. Let me look at what you're proposing and I'll see what I can do."

After meeting with Kae, Representative Justice decided to sponsor the domestic violence legislation.

"However," she told Kae, "I think this proposal may involve a lot of legal questions that will need to be addressed by the legislature's bill drafters. So

I'm going to explain to them what we're trying to do and leave the drafting to them, rather than giving them your version. I've followed that same procedure with my handgun bill."

Options after the Draft

When the draft of a proposal has been completed by the legislature's bill drafters it goes to the member who requested it. The next step in the process is up to the legislator, who has several options:

Decide not to introduce the bill. A member is not obligated to introduce legislation simply because a draft was requested. For example, between the time that Representative Margaret Justice requested a bill concerning domestic violence and the time the draft was completed she may have decided not to introduce it because she had determined that it would be controversial and not likely to pass.

Line up cosponsors. The legislator who originates a bill request is the prime sponsor, but there may be other members who are willing to have their names on the bill as cosponsors because they support the proposal. And if Representative Lyle Spahnser, for example, can persuade a significant number of House members to cosponsor his bill to prevent juvenile and gang-related crimes, he will have a better chance of getting it passed.

Prefile the bill. If the draft of a bill is completed before the beginning of the legislative session, it maybe prefiled. Senator Brian Caucus's bill authorizing counties to adopt ordinances concerning loitering, graffiti, and curfews was drafted before the opening day of the session. He prefiled it so that it would be introduced on the first day of the session, getting an early start in the legislative process.

Introducing Bills

When bills are introduced, it is said they are "tossed in the hopper." Bills can only be introduced during a session of the House or Senate, so the bills that Senator Caucus and Representatives Justice and Spahnser had prefiled were not officially introduced until the first day of the session. At that time they were given numbers and referred to committees.

In most state legislatures introduction and **referral** to a committee constitutes the "**first reading**" of a bill. First reading of a bill does not mean they are actually read at the time of introduction. The reading clerk in the House or Senate simply gives the number of the bill, the bill's sponsor and **title**, and the committee to which it is assigned. That constitutes "first reading."

SUMMARY

On paper, the law-making process is simple: introduction of a bill, committee consideration, floor action by both chambers of the legislature, final passage, and the governor's signature or veto. In practice, it is not quite so simple. The power structure—the leadership and the personalities of individual members—plays a major role in legislative bodies. An understanding of how legislatures really work is essential for anyone who wants to make a difference.

The process begins with an idea that is drafted into a bill. Theoretically, anyone may write a bill. Writing proposed legislation, however, requires specialized legal knowledge. That is why most bills are written by the legislature's staff attorneys who are experienced drafters. Bills drafted by anyone outside the legislature must be reviewed by the legislature's legal staff to ensure that they are in the correct form for bills.

The next step in the process is the actual introduction of a bill. Bills can be introduced only by members of the legislature—not by private citizens, or lobbyists, or even the governor or other state officials. Anyone other than a member who wants a bill introduced must persuade a legislator to sponsor it.

Bills can be introduced only when the legislature is in session. In most states, bills can be prefiled, but they are not officially introduced, given a number, and assigned to a committee until the legislative session begins.

Only the bill's title is read when it is introduced, but introduction normally constitutes "first reading." Most state legislatures require three "readings" of a bill for passage. The other two readings will be discussed in later chapters.

TABLE 5.1

MECHANISMS USED TO EXPEDITE AND STREAMLINE BILL PROCESSING

State	Prefiling Bills	Proposed Short-form, or Skeleton Bills	Companion Bills	Committee Bills	Carryover of Bills from 1st to 2nd Session of Biennium	Bill Introduction Limits	Bill Introduction Deadlines	Committee Action Deadlines	1st and 2nd House Action Deadlines
Alabama	B		B				S		
Alaska	B		B	B	B		B		
Arizona	B			B			B	B	B
Arkansas	B			B			B		
California	H		H	H	H	S	H	H	H
Colorado	B			S		B	B	B	B
Connecticut		B		B			B	B	
Delaware	B						H*	H	
Florida	B	H	B	B	H	H	B	H	
Georgia					B		B		S
Hawaii	B	B	H		B	H	B	B	B
Idaho				S	S		S		
Illinois	B			B			B	B	B
Indiana	B					B	B	B	B
Iowa	B	S	B	B	B		B	B	B
Kansas	B			B	B		B	H	H
Kentucky	B		B				B	B	
Louisiana	B			H			B		
Maine	B		H		B		B	B	
Maryland	B		S	B			B	B	B
Massachusetts	B		S	B			B	B	
Michigan			S			B	S	B	
Minnesota	H	H	B	B	B	B		B	H
Mississippi	B			B			B	B	B
Missouri	B		S				B		
Montana	B			B		B	B	B	B
Nebraska	S			S	S		S		
Nevada	B	B				B	(1)		
New Hampshire	B				H		B	H	B
New Jersey	B		B	S			S		
New Mexico	B						B		H
New York	B		B		B		B	B	B
North Carolina	B	B	B	B	B		B	H	B

TABLE 5.1 (CONTINUED)

Mechanisms Used to Expedite and Streamline Bill Processing

State	Prefiling Bills	Proposed Short-form, or Skeleton Bills	Companion Bills	Committee Bills	Carryover of Bills from 1st to 2nd Session of Biennium	Bill Introduction Limits	Bill Introduction Deadlines	Committee Action Deadlines	1st and 2nd House Action Deadlines
North Dakota	B			B		B	B	B	B
Ohio	B				B				B
Oklahoma	B				B		B	B	B
Oregon	B			B	B		B	B	
Pennsylvania	S				S				
Rhode Island	**								
South Carolina	B	H	B	S	B		S	H	
South Dakota	B			B	B		B	B	B
Tennessee	B		B	S	B	S	B		
Texas	B		S	B			B		
Utah	B	H		B			B	H	
Vermont	B	H	S	H	B		B	H	
Virginia	B				B		B	B	
Washington	B		S		B		S	B	B
West Virginia	B		H	H	B		B	H	B
Wisconsin			H		H				
Wyoming	B		H	B			B		B

Key:
B = Both chambers
S = Senate or Council only
H = House or Assembly only
* = During 2nd session of biennium only
** = Did not respond to survey

Notes:
1. In Nevada, legislation requested by any state agency or local government must be drafted by the first day of the legislative session and must be introduced within 15 legislative days. Any state agency or local government bill not drafted before the first legislative day may be introduced only during the 15 legislative days following delivery of the bill draft. Members must place their requests for drafts of bills or joint resolutions prior to the 11th calendar day; however, there is no deadline as to when the bill or joint resolution may be introduced.

TABLE 5.2

READING OF BILLS—SENATE

State	How Many Readings Required?	Must Readings Be on Separate Days?	When is a Bill Required to be Read in Full?				
			1st Reading	2nd Reading	3rd Reading	Final Passage	Never
Alabama	3	Yes			X		
Alaska	3	Yes					X
Arizona	3	Yes					X
Arkansas	3	Yes					X
California	No response						
Colorado	3	Yes					X
Connecticut	3	Yes					X
Delaware	3	2nd, 3rd rdgs					X
Florida	3	Yes					X
Georgia	3	Yes					On order
Hawaii	3	Yes					X
Idaho	3	Yes	X*	X*	X*		
Illinois	3	Yes					X
Indiana	3	Yes					X
Iowa	2	No					X
Kansas	3	Yes					X
Kentucky	3	No	X*	X*	X*		
Louisiana	3	Yes					X
Maine	2	Yes	X*	X*			
Maryland	3	Yes					X
Massachusetts	3	Yes					X
Michigan	3	Yes					X
Minnesota	3	Yes					X
Mississippi	3	Yes					X
Missouri	3	Yes	**				
Montana	3	Yes					X
Nebraska	4	Yes				X	
Nevada	3	Yes		X*	X*	X*	
New Hampshire	3	No					X
New Jersey	3	No					X
New Mexico	3	Yes	X*	X*	X*		
New York	3	No					X
North Carolina	3	Yes					X
North Dakota	2	Yes					X
Ohio	3	Yes					X
Oklahoma	3	Yes	**				
Oregon	3	Yes			X*	X*	
Pennsylvania	3	Yes					X
Rhode Island	No response						
South Carolina	3	Yes		X*			
South Dakota	2	Yes					X
Tennessee	3	Yes					X
Texas	3	Yes	X*	X*	X*		
Utah	3	Yes					X
Vermont	3	Yes					X
Virginia	3	No					X
Washington	3	No		X*			
West Virginia	3	Yes			X*		
Wisconsin	3	Yes					X
Wyoming	3	Yes					X

* However, a full reading typically does not occur.
**Did not respond to survey.

TABLE 5.3

READING OF BILLS—HOUSE

State	How Many Readings Required?	Must Readings Be on Separate Days?	When is a Bill Required to be Read in Full?				
			1st Reading	2nd Reading	3rd Reading	Final Passage	Never
Alabama	3	Yes			X		
Alaska	3	Yes					X
Arizona	3	Yes					X
Arkansas	3	Yes	X	X	X		
California	3	Yes					X
Coloraoo	3	Yes					X
Connecticut	3	Yes					X
Delaware	3	Yes					X
Florida	3	Yes					X
Georgia	3	Yes					X
Hawaii	3	Yes					X
Idaho	No response						
Illinois	3	Yes					X
Indiana	3	Yes	**				
Iowa	3	Yes					X
Kansas	3	Yes					X
Kentucky	3	Yes	X*				
Louisiana	3	Yes					X
Maine	2	No					X
Maryland	3	Yes					X
Massachusetts	3	Yes					on request
Michigan	3	No			X		
Minnesota	3	Yes					X
Mississippi	3	Yes				on request	
Missouri	3	Yes	**				
Montana	3	Yes					X
Nebraska	Not appＩable—unicanＩal legislaＩre						
Nevada	3	Yes		X*	X*	X*	
New Hampshire	3	No					X
New Jersey	3	Yes					X
New Mexico	3	Yes					X
New York	3	Yes					X
North Carolina	3	Yes					X
North Dakota	2	Yes					X
Ohio	3	Yes					X
Oklahoma	3	Yes	**				
Oregon	3	Yes			X*	X*	
Pennsylvania	3	Yes					X
Rhode Island	No response						
South Carolina	3	Yes					X
South Dakota	2	Yes					X
Tennessee	3	Yes					X
Texas	3	Yes					X
Utah	3	No					X
Vermont	3	Yes					X
Virginia	3	Yes					X
Washington	3	Yes		X*			
West Virginia	3	Yes	X*	X*	X*		
Wisconsin	3	Yes					X
Wyoming	3	Yes					X

* However, a full reading typically does not occur.
**Did not respond to survey.

PART

III

The Legislative
Process

CHAPTER

•••••••••

Committees

Committees are the heart of the legislative process. Much of the work of legislative bodies takes place during committee consideration of bills, and it is only during committee hearings that nonlegislators have an opportunity to speak on proposed legislation. In this chapter we will learn what happened in committee to the six bills that were introduced by Senator Brian Caucus and Representatives Margaret Justice and Lyle Spahnser.

C ommittees are the heart of the state and federal legislative process. They are the place where the legislature does its homework. During committee consideration, members have an opportunity to hear from supporters and opponents of a bill, to look closely at the details of proposed legislation, to give thoughtful consideration to proposed amendments, and to acquire considerable information about the subject—in short, to become knowledgeable enough to make an informed decision on whether to vote for or against a proposal.

Committee hearings also fulfill another significant function: they provide individual citizens and groups an opportunity to express formally, in a public forum, their views on proposed legislation. Committee hearings, in fact, are the only time during the legislative process when individuals or groups have that opportunity. When a proposed bill moves to the floor of a legislative chamber for debate and voting, only members are allowed to speak.

There are other ways, of course, that individuals, associations, or special interest groups can voice their opinions on pending legislation. They can talk to individual legislators, they can mount letter-writing and telephone campaigns to legislators, and they can provide legislators with summaries of their position on proposed legislation. But their only opportunity for discussion in a public forum is during committee hearings.

For example, if Megan McNally, the high school student who was introduced in the opening case study, wants to voice her opinions about the need for more state funding for public schools—in support of the supplemental funding requested by Governor Martinez—she will be able to do so at a hearing of the Senate or House Appropriations committee. Following the advice of her lobbyist friend, Frank Thorne, Megan may also employ several other lobbying methods to influence the legislature's decision concerning the funding of public schools. She may organize a letter-writing and telephone campaign in an attempt to influence legislators—getting parents, fellow students, teachers, and school administrators to join in the effort to get additional funding for public schools.

THE COMMITTEE STRUCTURE

There are four basic types of committees in state legislatures: **standing, interim, select,** and **joint**. Both standing and select committees are found in the U.S. Congress, but not **interim committees** because in Congress there is no interim: the U.S. Congress is in session throughout the year, and studies of proposed legislation or specific policy questions are conducted by existing Congressional committees or subcommittees. State legislatures use interim committees to study public policy questions in the time between the conclusion of a legislative session and the beginning of the next session (the *interim* between the sessions).

Interim committees are usually established for a single purpose, i.e., to study a specific subject during the interim between legislative sessions and make recommendations regarding legislation to be considered in the ensuing session. Interim committees may be composed of members of both legislative chambers and, occasionally, may also include persons who are not members of the legislature. Interim committees dissolve when they have fulfilled their charge to study a specific subject, and they play no role—other than through their recommendations—in the legislative process.

Select committees are similar to interim committees, except that they conduct their business during a legislative session. Their sole purpose, as with interim committees, is to consider and make recommendations on specific proposals.

Some legislatures also utilize joint committees, usually with members from both chambers and sometimes with nonlegislators. The purpose of joint committees is to reduce House versus Senate conflict as well as make more efficient use of the time of the legislature, executive branch agencies, and lobbyists by reducing the necessity for duplicate hearings in each chamber. And since members from both chambers serve on joint committees, they become familiar with the details of proposals before these proposals are brought before each chamber. The members of the joint committee also are able to serve as sources of information for their colleagues when the proposal is considered by the House and Senate. Three states—Connecticut, Massachusetts, and Maine—use joint committees almost exclusively to hear and consider legislative proposals. Fifteen states have joint budget or appropriations committees to streamline that process.

Standing committees are the legislature's workhorses. Unlike interim and select committees, standing committees have a continuing responsibility in a general field of legislative activity such as education, transportation, banking, appropriations, or taxation. Bills introduced during a session are normally assigned to the standing committee responsible for considering and acting on legislation in the bill's subject area.

The number of standing committees and their names vary from state to state, and within states from chamber to chamber. Each legislative chamber establishes that chamber's standing committees. Following a general election, two years in most states but four years in some, the legislature may alter the standing committee structure by creating new committees, eliminating others, or combining two or more. Generally, however, few changes are made; the standing committees that existed in previous sessions are continued. Standing committees are as close as you can come to finding permanent fixtures in the structure of state legislative bodies.

What does change following a general election, however, is the membership of the standing committees. The political party that wins a majority of seats in a legislative chamber controls the number of members, and their party affiliation, on each committee. Let's say that a state has 80 members in the House of Representatives or its equivalent. In the general election the Republicans won 48 seats (60 percent of 80) and the Democrats won 32 (40 percent of 80). In the imaginary state we're using as an example, assume that it is customary for each standing committee to have 15 members. Given the election results (48 Republicans; 32 Democrats), there would be nine Republicans (60 percent of 15) and six Democrats (40 percent of 15) on every standing committee. And in this example, if the number of members on any standing committee varied from our hypothetical 15, the same ratio would still be applied: 60 percent of the members would be from the majority party; 40 percent from the minority party.

Among the 50 states there is a rich variety in the names of standing committees. Some, however, are common to many states. Those found most frequently include Education, Agriculture, Finance, Appropriations, Ways and Means, Judiciary, Environment/Natural Resources, Banking, Health/Welfare/Human Services, Business Affairs and Labor, Local Government, and Highways/Transportation. Their names suggest the field of legislative activity for which they are responsible. The exception might be Ways and Means which, literally, implies ways and means of raising revenues to fund state programs. In other words, tax measures.

COMMITTEE ACTION

After a standing committee has done its homework by holding public hearings and compiling information about a bill, committee members go over the proposed legislation in detail. At this stage, members of the committee may propose amendments they believe to be necessary to refine the bill or to achieve a particular purpose they favor. The committee may even rewrite significant portions of a bill. Only committee members may offer amendments, and votes are taken on each amendment. Once the public hearings are over, there is no further formal input from individual citizens, associations, or special interest groups.

When a committee has completed its deliberations and the bill has been amended or remains unchanged as introduced, a number of things can happen next.

- If no amendments were adopted and the majority of the committee is in agreement—a rare occasion on both counts—the committee can report a bill with a recommendation that it pass;
- A bill can be reported as amended, with a recommendation that it pass;
- A bill can be reported without recommendation;
- A bill can be reported with recommendation that it fail;
- The committee can vote to postpone the bill indefinitely. In most states that would amount to killing it. The committee can also vote to postpone a bill for a specific period of time.
- The committee can vote to kill the bill.

Those are the options that are generally available to standing commit-tees in a majority of the states. There may be other options, depending upon the state. As we have emphasized, it is rare to find two or more states that follow exactly the same procedures in anything they do. In a number of states, for example, a bill may be reported with a recommendation that it be referred to another committee, or with a recommendation that it be the subject of an interim study. And in some states, bills may be referred to more than one committee.

A statement that applies universally, however, is that the most influen-tial member of a committee is the chair. The chair sets the committee's agenda, determining when—and in many states whether—bills will be considered. With the exception of a few states, a **committee chair** may kill a bill by refusing to put it "on the table" for action by the full committee. There are procedures for forcing committee consideration of a bill, even with the chair's dissent, but they are used infrequently and even then are seldom successful. Legislators are often hesitant to incur the displeasure of a committee chair by attempting to force consideration of a bill over the objections of the chair.

It is frequently the case that in many legislative bodies a majority of the bills introduced never get out of committee. Recent sessions of the Wis-consin legislature are typical: 57 percent of the bills introduced never left the committee to which they were referred.

Based on the premise that the full membership of a legislative chamber should have an opportunity to vote on proposed legislation rather than allowing bills to be bottled up in committee, a few legislatures require committees to report all bills referred to them. There are 99 legislative chambers in the United States—two in each state except Nebraska, which has only one chamber. Committees in 21 legislative chambers must report all bills referred to them. In Colorado, Maine, Massachusetts, New Hamp-shire, North Dakota, South Dakota, and Utah, both House and Senate committees must report on all bills. In Idaho, Illinois, and Maryland, Senate committees must report. In Arkansas, California, Indiana, and North Carolina, only the House committees must report on all bills. That leaves 78 legislative chambers—a significant number—in which there is no requirement that bills referred to committee must be reported to the House or Senate in order to ensure that all the members have an opportu-nity to vote on proposed legislation.

THE FATE OF SIX BILLS

Senator Brian Caucus and Representatives Lyle Spahnser and Margaret Justice sponsored the following six bills that were officially introduced on the first day of the session: Senate Bill 21 and Senate Bill 155, both by Senator Brian Caucus; House Bill 15 and House Bill 38, by Representative Margaret Justice, and House Bills 20 and 107, by Representative Spahnser.

Senate Bill 155

Senate Bill 155, by Brian Caucus, has the best chance of passage of any of the six bills we will be following. It was requested by Governor Vito Martinez and provides for a supplemental appropriation of $25 million for public schools. Brian Caucus, chair of the Senate Appropriations committee, scheduled an early hearing so that Senate Bill 155 could be voted up or down in the first days of the session, thus avoiding potential problems toward the end of the session when the legislature's calendar can jam up with last minute bill considerations.

Megan McNally, on the advice of her lobbyist friend, Frank Thorne, decided to testify at the Senate appropriations committee hearings on Senate Bill 155.

At the scheduled public hearing, Senator Caucus called the committee to order and recognized individuals who had requested to testify. The first asked to present testimony was Megan McNally. Following Frank Thorne's advice, she had prepared a brief statement and provided copies for each member of the committee.

"Mr. Chairman, members of the committee, my name is Megan McNally. I am a junior at Middle Park High school. I want to express my support of Senate Bill 155 that provides for an additional $25 million of state funds for public schools. You may be interested to know that I am expressing not only my views but those of a number of students in six other high schools in the metro area: Grandview, South Park, Jefferson, Ramsey, Woodlawn, and Central. These seven high schools have approximately 15,000 students. I don't want to imply that my testimony represents the views of every student, of course, but I have talked to a representative number of students in each of those high schools.

"We realize that there may be times when the state has little or no choice, but when you reduce state funding for public schools it is the students in every school who are most affected. Decreased state support means larger class sizes, fewer staff, and reductions in or, in some cases, elimination of programs that enrich a school's curriculum—programs like art and music, for example, and perhaps some vocational offerings.

"I have to admit that I first became interested in this subject when the school board in my district eliminated girls' basketball because of reduced state funding—and as a member of our team I was looking forward to a great season. As much as I may hate to admit it, I realize that the sky will not fall if we don't have a girls' basketball team this year. But the programs I have mentioned, plus some others I may have left out, do make a difference in the total educational picture.

"Mr. Chairman and members of the committee, I appreciate the oppor-tunity to present this testimony, and again, we urge your support of at least $25 million in additional state funding for public schools."

When the committee had heard from everyone who wanted to testify on Senate Bill 155 and had an opportunity to ask questions, Senator Caucus put the bill on the table for amendments and committee action. Senator Laurel Smith offered an amendment to increase the appropriation from $25 million to $40 million.

"I support that amendment," Senator Caucus said. "After the governor submitted this request, the State Budget Office issued a revised estimate of revenues for this year. Higher retail sales than were originally predicted will produce significantly more money from the state sales tax than anyone had expected," he explained, "so it appears there should be no problem with increasing the funding in this bill."

After adopting the Smith amendment and several minor technical amendments the committee voted to report the bill to the Senate, with a recommendation that it pass as amended.

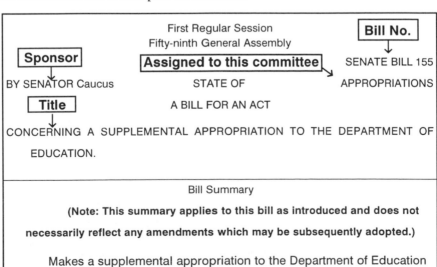

First Regular Session
Fifty-ninth General Assembly

Bill No.

Sponsor

Assigned to this committee

SENATE BILL 155

BY SENATOR Caucus

STATE OF

APPROPRIATIONS

Title

A BILL FOR AN ACT

CONCERNING A SUPPLEMENTAL APPROPRIATION TO THE DEPARTMENT OF EDUCATION.

Bill Summary

(Note: This summary applies to this bill as introduced and does not necessarily reflect any amendments which may be subsequently adopted.)

Makes a supplemental appropriation to the Department of Education

1 *Be it enacted by the General Assembly of the State:* ← **Enacting Clause**

2   **SECTION 1.** Part IV of section 2 of chapter 354, Session Laws of

3 1996, is amended to read:

4   SECTION 2. **Appropriation.**

5 **(1) Public School Finance**

6	Item & Subtotal	Total	General Fund
7 For General Programs, K-12	~~1,416,475,360~~		~~1,393,945,319~~
8	1,441,475,360		1,441,475,360
9 Public School Transportation	~~33,760,204~~		~~33,760,204~~
10	35,260,204		35,260,204
11 English Language Proficiency	3,139,180		3,139,180
12 Education of Exceptional			
13 Children	89,252,605		89,252,605
14			1,542,627,349
15		1,569,127,349	

16   **SECTION 2.** This bill shall take effect July 1, 1996.

Capital letters indicate new material to be added to existing statute.

Dashes through the words indicate deletions from existing statute.

Senate Bill 21

When testimony was completed on a supplemental appropriation for the Department of Education, Senator Caucus turned the committee hearing over to the vice-chair, Senator Mary Archuleta, and hurried to the hearing room where the Local Government committee was meeting. He had asked the chair to schedule a hearing on his bill granting counties the power to adopt ordinances discouraging loitering and graffiti, and imposing curfews.

Following customary procedure, Senator Doris Brooks, chair of the Local Government committee, recognized Senator Caucus—the bill's sponsor—first.

"Madam chair and members of the committee," he said, "this is a straightforward, uncomplicated bill, and I will not take up your time by going on at length. I just hope that you will support it. It merely says to counties: 'Here is the authority to do something about the problems associated with juvenile delinquency.' This bill does not require counties to do anything. But it does give them the authority to address their concerns if they feel it necessary to do so. I agreed to sponsor this legislation after hearing from a number of county commissioners who are experiencing problems in this area. And let me say that juvenile delinquency is not confined to the metropolitan areas of our state. Unfortunately, juvenile delinquency can be as much of a problem in less populous areas as it is in the big cities.

"As I said," he continued, "this is a simple, straightforward bill. It adds a new paragraph to the statutes relating to the powers granted to county commissioners.

"The new paragraph allows counties to adopt ordinances 'to discourage juvenile delinquency through the imposition of curfews applicable to juveniles, the restraint and punishment of loitering by juveniles, and the restraint and punishment of defacement of, including the affixing of graffiti to, buildings and other public or private property by juveniles.'

"That's it, it's that simple," Senator Caucus said. "The only thing I can add is that this bill has the support of the County Commissioners' Association. I trust that the committee will report it favorably for floor consideration. I would also like to introduce David Lam, director of the County Commissioners' Association, who is here to testify in support of this bill."

"Mr. Lam, the committee will be pleased to hear your comments on this legislation," Senator Brooks said.

"Thank you, Senator, I appreciate the opportunity to present the views of the counties," Lam responded.

"Madam chair and members of the committee," he continued, "as I'm sure you know, the County Commissioners' Association is an organization that represents every county in the state. When legislation affecting the counties is proposed, we make an analysis of the proposal and advise our members of its affect on county government and ask for their comments.

"Following that, we ask the position of each county, that is, whether they support or oppose the legislation and also whether they would like to see any changes in the bill as introduced. Our executive committee then decides what the Association's position will be on the legislation. That is our standard procedure.

"As you might expect," Lam continued, "reaching unanimous agreement among all the state's county governments is not something that happens frequently. That is why I'm pleased to advise you that with Senate

Bill 21 there was no disagreement from any county in the state about the need for this legislation as introduced by Senator Caucus. As Senator Caucus said in his testimony, juvenile delinquency is not a problem that is confined to the urban areas of our state. It is a problem that touches communities and counties throughout our state. This bill is not a cure-all, of course, but it will give county governments another tool to use, if they so choose, in their efforts to control juvenile crime and delinquency. We urge your support of Senate Bill 21."

"We appreciate having the views of your association, Mr. Lam," Senator Brooks said. "Are there questions from the committee?" There were none.

After hearing from several other witnesses, all of whom spoke in favor of the bill, Senator Brooks said, "The bill is on the table. What is the committee's pleasure?"

"Madam chair," Senator Lackey said, "I would like to offer an amendment. It is a very minor, technical amendment that will in no way change the substance or the intent of the legislation.

"My amendment reads as follows: on page 1, lines 12 and 13, after the word 'punishment' delete the word 'of' and **insert** the word 'for.'" The Lackey amendment was seconded by Senator Weissmann.

"Madam chair," Senator Lackey said, "I move the **adoption** of my amendment. As I said, it is a very minor amendment. I offer it only because the language of the bill as introduced seems clumsy at that particular point, and I think the members would agree with me if they read it carefully. All this amendment does is substitute the word 'for' for the word 'of' in order to make the language clearer and more readable."

"Is there further discussion of the Lackey amendment to Senate Bill 21?" Senator Brooks said. "Is there objection to the adoption of the amendment?" she added. "Hearing none, the Lackey amendment to Senate Bill 21 is adopted.

"If there are no further amendments and no further discussion, the chair will entertain a **motion** on Senate Bill 21," Senator Brooks said.

"I move the adoption of Senate Bill 21 as amended, with a recommendation that it **do pass**," Senator Lackey said.

On a roll-call vote, the Local Government committee voted unanimously to report the bill, as amended, with a recommendation that it pass.

First Regular Session
Fifty-ninth General Assembly

SENATE BILL 21

STATE OF

BY SENATOR Caucus

LOCAL GOVERNMENT

A BILL FOR AN ACT
CONCERNING THE POWER OF COUNTIES TO ADOPT ORDINANCES
RELATING TO JUVENILE ACTIVITIES.

Bill Summary

(Note: This summary applies to this bill as introduced and does not necessarily reflect any amendments which may be subsequently adopted.)

Grants counties additional powers to adopt ordinances relating to juvenile curfews, loitering by juveniles, and placement of graffiti by juveniles.

1
2 *Be it enacted by the General Assembly of the State:*
3 **SECTION 1**. 30-15-401 (1), Revised Statutes, 1986 Repl. Vol., as
4 amended, is amended BY THE ADDITION OF A NEW PARAGRAPH to read:
5 **30-15-401. General regulations**. (1) In addition to those powers
6 granted by sections 30-11-101 and 30-11-107 and by parts 1, 2, and 3 of
7 this article, the board of county commissioners has the power to adopt
8 ordinances for control or licensing of those matters of purely local concern
9 which are described in the following enumerated powers:
10 (d.5) TO DISCOURAGE JUVENILE DELINQUENCY THROUGH THE
11 IMPOSITION OF CURFEWS APPLICABLE TO JUVENILES, THE RESTRAINT
12 AND PUNISHMENT OF LOITERING BY JUVENILES, AND THE RESTRAINT
13 AND PUNISHMENT OF DEFACEMENT OF, INCLUDING THE AFFIXING OF
14 GRAFFITI TO, BUILDINGS AND OTHER PUBLIC OR PRIVATE PROPERTY
15 BY JUVENILES. FOR PURPOSES OF THIS PARAGRAPH (d.5), "JUVENILE"
16 MEANS A JUVENILE AS DEFINED IN SECTION 19-2-101 (7).

1   **SECTION 2. Safety clause**. The general assembly hereby finds, deter- 2 mines, and declares that this act is necessary for the immediate preservation 3 of the public peace, health, and safety.

Capital letters indicate new material to be added to existing statute. *Dashes through the words indicate deletions from existing statute.*

House Bill 15

Now we move to the House where we will follow four bills, but not in as much detail as the two Senate bills we followed. The procedural consideration of bills in committee is essentially the same in both chambers. We will be looking at two bills sponsored by Representative Margaret Justice and two by Representative Lyle Spahnser.

House Bill 15, by Representative Justice, was assigned to the Judiciary committee. Her bill involves a prohibition on the sale of firearms. At the committee hearing she explained that the bill bans the sale of any firearm, except for shotguns or rifles, to any person under 21 and prohibits the sale of all firearms, including shotguns and rifles, to anyone under 18.

"My bill," Representative Justice said, "presents an opportunity for us to do something about the increasing violence by juveniles, with which we are all familiar. It will keep guns out of the hands of young gang members.

"Statistics from every law enforcement agency in this state and other states throughout the country show that violent crimes among juveniles, especially violent crimes involving the use of handguns, are soaring," Representative Justice said. "You can place the blame for that wherever it suits you—on the dramatic increase in single-parent families, on the welfare system, on the lack of family values, on the school system, on TV and Hollywood movies that celebrate violence—whatever coincides with your philosophy.

"But whatever rationale you choose will not change the facts. The easy availability of handguns has contributed to the phenomenal increase in juvenile crimes involving guns in the past 10 years," Representative Justice said. "And I will tell you in advance," she continued, "that I don't buy the argument I'm sure the gun lobby will make that this bill violates the Second Amendment to the U.S. Constitution. I hope the committee will report this bill favorably so that the full membership of the House, and subsequently the Senate if it passes in the House, will have an opportunity to vote on this most important issue."

"We appreciate having your testimony," the chairman of the Judiciary committee, Representative Phil Lowery, responded. "Are there questions? Representative Williams."

"Representative Justice," Williams said, "you've made a good case for this bill. However, I do have some reservations about the constitutionality of this legislation. The Second Amendment to the U.S. Constitution says, and I quote: 'A well regulated Militia, being necessary to the security of a free State, the right of the people to keep and bear Arms, shall not be infringed.' Now how does that square with your bill, which says that anyone under 18 would not be allowed to buy any kind of firearm, not just handguns?"

"Representative Williams, I think it comes down to a matter of interpreting the Second Amendment in the context of the times," Representative Justice replied. "The Second Amendment was added to the Constitution more than 200 years ago, not long after 'A well regulated Militia' played a major role in the struggle of the colonies for independence from what many felt was dictatorial and repressive government rule. But that was in the eighteenth century. Times have changed. The freedom and the rights of individuals that we all value so highly are not dependent, in today's world, on the 'well regulated Militia' referred to in the Second Amendment."

Frank Thorne, a lobbyist for the state chapter of the National Rifle Association, the state Outfitters and Guides Association, and the state Association of Licensed Firearms Dealers, gave the views of his clients.

"We appreciate Representative Justice's position," he said. "At the same time, we have some real concerns about the constitutionality of this legislation. The Second Amendment to the U.S. Constitution guarantees citizens the right to bear arms. It doesn't say 'except for handguns,' and it doesn't say 'except for citizens under 18.' So we oppose the whole bill on those grounds. However, given the possibility that this bill may be reported, we would suggest that it be amended to allow the sale of shotguns or rifles to anyone under 18 who has passed a certified course on firearm safety. That would take care of some of our objections to this legislation, because it would allow young people an opportunity to own firearms for hunting purposes."

The amendment suggested by Frank Thorne was offered by Representative Williams and was adopted on a roll-call vote.

After further discussion, the committee voted, 6-5, to report the bill to the House, as amended and without recommendation.

First Regular Session
Fifty-ninth General Assembly

HOUSE BILL 15

BY REPRESENTATIVE Justice   STATE OF   JUDICIARY

A BILL FOR AN ACT
CONCERNING THE CREATION OF THE CRIME OF UNLAWFUL
SALE OF A FIREARM.

Bill Summary

(Note: This summary applies to this bill as introduced and does not necessarily reflect any amendments which may be subsequently adopted.)

Creates the crime of unlawful sale of a firearm and establishes a penalty therefor.

1 Be it enacted by the General Assembly of the State:
2   **SECTION 1.** Article 12 of title 18, Revised Statutes, 1986 Repl. Vol.,
3 as amended, is amended by the ADDITION OF A NEW SECTION to read:
4   **18-12-107.9. Unlawful sale of a firearm - penalty.**
5 (1) NO PERSON, INCLUDING ANY LICENSED DEALER, LICENSED IM-
6 PORTER, OR LICENSED MANUFACTURER WHO IS LICENSED PURSU-
7 ANT TO 18 U.S.C. SEC. 923, SHALL SELL ANY FIREARM, OTHER THAN
8 A SHOTGUN OR RIFLE, TO ANY PERSON UNDER THE AGE OF TWENTY-
9 ONE YEARS. NO PERSON, INCLUDING ANY LICENSED DEALER, LI-
10 CENSED IMPORTER, OR LICENSED MANUFACTURER WHO IS LI-
11 CENSED PURSUANT TO U.S.C. SEC. 923, SHALL SELL ANY SHOTGUN
12 OR RIFLE TO ANY PERSON UNDER THE AGE OF EIGHTEEN YEARS.
13   (2) ANY PERSON WHO SELLS ANY TYPE OF FIREARM IN VIOLA-
14 TION OF SUBSECTION (1) OF THIS SECTION COMMITS THE OFFENSE
15 OF UNLAWFUL SALE OF A FIREARM.
16   (3) UNLAWFUL SALE IS A CLASS 1 MISDEMEANOR.
17   **SECTION 2. Effective date - applicability.** This act shall take effect
18 upon passage and shall apply to offenses committed on or after said
19 date.

Capital letters indicate new material to be added to existing statute.
Dashes through the words indicate deletions from existing statute.

House Bill 38

The second of Representative Justice's bills, the domestic violence legislation suggested by Kae Kittredge, was also referred to the Judiciary committee.

"This bill would go a long way toward providing protection to women who suffer physical abuse by their spouses," Representative Justice told the committee. "Domestic violence is a problem that society would like to pretend doesn't exist. Unfortunately, it does, and this legislation addresses the problem by providing at least some degree of protection to women who suffer abuse. It would mandate the arrest of abusers, even though the spouse refused to sign a complaint, and the alleged abuser would have to spend at least one night in jail and post bond to be released. It also provides for better enforcement of restraining orders by requiring police officers to notify a protected party of a violation of a restraining order. I urge the committee to give favorable consideration to this bill," Representative Justice said.

In questioning following her testimony, several committee members indicated they were sympathetic to what Representative Justice was trying to accomplish with her bill, but said they could not support mandatory arrests. "I just have a hard time requiring an arrest when the spouse is not willing to sign a complaint," one committee member commented. "And I question whether an arrest under those circumstances would stand up to a court challenge."

"Mr. Chairman, and members of the committee," Representative Justice said, "I would like to respond to the question that has been raised concerning the mandate for peace officers to arrest an alleged abuser, even though the victim may not be willing to sign a complaint.

"The bill says," Representative Justice continued, "that when a peace officer has probable cause to believe a crime involving domestic violence has been committed, the officer shall arrest the person suspected of its commission and charge the person with the crime, whether or not the alleged victim wishes to pursue the filing of charges.

"So we are giving the police the right to charge an alleged abuser. I cannot say to you, of course, that the section I have quoted would be upheld by the courts if there were a challenge. But I can tell you that the procedure outlined in my bill has been followed for several years by the police in several local jurisdictions, and to date it has not been challenged."

Even with Representative Justice's defense of her bill and after considerable discussion, the committee voted 7-4 to kill the bill.

First Regular Session
Fifty-ninth General Assembly

HOUSE BILL 38

BY REPRESENTATIVE Justice   STATE OF

JUDICIARY

A BILL FOR AN ACT

CONCERNING STATUTORY PROVISIONS TO REDUCE THE INCIDENCE
OF DOMESTIC VIOLENCE.

Bill Summary

(Note: This summary applies to this bill as introduced and does not necessarily reflect any amendments which may be subsequently adopted.)

Increases the crime of violation of a restraining order to a class 2 misdemeanor and requires a mandatory minimum sentence. Enhances the penalty if a person has previously been convicted of violating a restraining order. Mandates a peace officer to arrest a person who the officer has probable cause to believe has committed a crime involving domestic violence or has violated a restraining order or emergency protection order. Authorizes a court issuing a restraining order to prevent domestic abuse to grant parenting time with certain conditions, including supervision of such parenting time. Requires a restraining order to prevent domestic abuse to be served personally upon the defendant. Prohibits a court from denying such a restraining order solely due to a lapse in time between an act of domestic abuse and the filing of the petition for the restraining order. Permits a court to make a temporary order to prevent domestic abuse permanent upon default, without further notice or service of process, if the responding party fails to appear at the show cause hearing.

Directs a peace officer to use every reasonable means to protect a person protected by a restraining order, including but not limited to transporting the person and such person's minor child to shelter. Requires a peace officer to arrest an alleged violator for violation of a restraining order and transport such person to jail.

Authorizes the restriction of a criminal defendant's calling privileges from a jail or correctional facility if such defendant's alleged victim is able to demonstrate the violation of a restraining order.

1 *Be it enacted by the General Assembly of the State:*

2   **SECTION 1.** 18-6-803.5, 1986 Repl. Vol., as amended, is amended

3 to read:

4   **18-6-803.5. Crime of violation of a restraining order - penalty.** (2)

1 Violation of a restraining order is a class ~~3~~ 2 misdemeanor, ~~when the~~
2 ~~court order violated has been issued pursuant to section 13-6-107,~~
3 ~~sections 14-4-101 to 14-4-104, the portions of section 14-10-108, autho~~
4 ~~rizing the restraining and enjoining of any person from threatening,~~
5 ~~beating, striking, or assaulting any other person or requiring a person to~~
6 ~~leave certain premises, rule 365 of the rules of county court civil proce~~
7 ~~dure, any protective order issued pursuant to title 19, or a municipal~~
8 ~~ordinance which provides for an order to issue which restrains any~~
9 ~~person from threatening, molesting, or injuring any person, or entering or~~
10 ~~remaining on the premises. However, when it is plead and proven that~~
11 ~~the violator has been previously convicted within seven years under this~~
12 ~~section, the offense is a class 1 misdemeanor.~~ AND, IN ADDITION TO
13 ANY OTHER PENALTY, ANY PERSON CONVICTED OF SUCH OF
14 FENSE SHALL BE SENTENCED TO A MANDATORY MINIMUM SEN-
15 TENCE OF SIXTY DAYS IMPRISONMENT IN THE COUNTY JAIL. IF THE
16 RESTRAINED PERSON HAS PREVIOUSLY BEEN CONVICTED OF VIO-
17 LATING THIS SECTION OR A FORMER VERSION OF THIS SECTION
18 OR A CONCURRENT MUNICIPAL ORDINANCE, SUCH PERSON COM-
19 MITS A CLASS Q MISDEMEANOR AND, IN ADDITION TO ANY OTHER
20 PENALTY, SHALL BE SENTENCED TO A MANDATORY MINIMUM SEN-
21 TENCE OF ONE HUNDRED TWENTY DAYS IMPRISONMENT IN THE
22 COUNTY JAIL. IF THE RESTRAINED PERSON HAS PREVIOUSLY BEEN
23 CONVICTED TWO OR MORE TIMES OF VIOLATING THIS SECTION OR
24 A FORMER VERSION OF THIS SECTION OR AN ANALOGOUS MUNICI-
25 PAL ORDINANCE, SUCH PERSON COMMITS A CLASS 1 MISDE-
26 MEANOR AND, IN ADDITION TO ANY OTHER PENALTY, SHALL BE
27 SENTENCED TO A MANDATORY MINIMUM SENTENCE OF ONE HUN-
28 DRED EIGHTY DAYS IMPRISONMENT IN THE COUNTY JAIL. Nothing
29 in this subsection shall preclude the ability of a municipality to enact
30 concurrent ordinances. Any sentence imposed pursuant to this subsec-
31 tion shall run consecutively and not concurrently with any sentence
32 imposed for any crime which gave rise to the issuing of the restraining
33 order.

Capital letters indicate new material to be added to existing statute.
Dashes through the words indicate deletions from existing statute.

1 **SECTION 2.** Part 8 of article 6 of title 18, 1986 Repl. Vol., as amended
2 is amended BY THE ADDITION OF THE FOLLOWING NEW SECTIONS
3 to read:

4 **18.6.803.7. Duties of peace officers and prosecuting agencies -**
5 **preservation of evidence.** (1) WHEN A PEACE OFFICER DETERMINES
6 THAT THERE IS PROBABLE CAUSE TO BELIEVE THAT A CRIME
7 INVOLVING DOMESTIC VIOLENCE HAS BEEN COMMITTED, THE OF-
8 FICER SHALL ARREST THE PERSON SUSPECTED OF ITS COMMIS-
9 SION AND CHARGE THE PERSON WITH THE APPROPRIATE CRIME,
10 REGARDLESS OF WHETHER OR NOT THE ALLEGED VICTIM WISHES
11 TO PURSUE THE FILING OF CHARGES AGAINST SUCH PERSON.

12 (a) A PEACE OFFICER SHALL USE EVERY REASONABLE MEANS TO
13 PROTECT THE PERSON OR PERSONS PROTECTED BY A RESTRAIN-
14 ING ORDER AND TO PREVENT FURTHER VIOLENCE INCLUDING, BUT
15 NOT LIMITED TO, TRANSPORTING, OR OBTAINING TRANSPORTA-
16 TION FOR, THE VICTIM TO SHELTER. UPON THE REQUEST OF THE
17 PROTECTED PERSON, THE PEACE OFFICER MAY ALSO TRANSPORT
18 THE MINOR CHILD OF THE PROTECTED PERSON, WHO IS NOT AN
19 EMANCIPATED MINOR, TO THE SAME SHELTER IF SUCH SHELTER IS
20 WILLING TO ACCEPT THE CHILD.

21 (b) FOR PURPOSES OF THIS SUBSECTION, "SHELTER" MEANS A
22 BATTERED WOMEN'S SHELTER, A FRIEND'S OR FAMILY MEMBER'S
23 HOME, OR SUCH OTHER SAFE HAVEN AS MAY BE DESIGNATED BY
24 THE PROTECTED PERSON AND WHICH IS WITHIN A REASONABLE
25 DISTANCE FROM THE LOCATION AT WHICH THE PEACE OFFICER
26 FOUND THE VICTIM.

27 **SECTION 3.** 14-4-102 (2) (d) (II), (4), (6), and (7.5), 1987 Repl. Vol.,
28 as amended, are amended, and the said 14-4-102 is further amended
29 BY THE ADDITION OF THE FOLLOWING NEW SUBSECTIONS, to
30 read:

31 **14-4-102. Restraining orders to prevent domestic abuse.** (2) A
32 temporary or permanent restraining order to prevent domestic abuse
33 may include:

34 (d) (II) If temporary care and control is awarded, the order may
35 include parenting time rights for the other party involved PURSUANT
36 TO SECTION 14-10-129 AND ANY CONDITIONS OF SUCH
37 PARENTING TIME, INCLUDING THE SUPERVISION OF SUCH

1 PARENTING TIME BY A THIRD PARTY WHO AGREES ON THE
2 RECORD TO THE TERMS OF THE SUPERVISED PARENTING TIME.
3 THE RESTRAINED PARTY SHALL BE ORDERED TO PAY THE COSTS,
4 IF ANY, ASSOCIATED WITH THE SUPERVISED PARENTING TIME IF
5 HE OR SHE IS FINANCIALLY CAPABLE. IF THE COURT FINDS THAT
6 THE SAFETY OF ANY CHILD OR THE PROTECTED PARTY CANNOT BE
7 ENSURED WITH ANY FORM OF PARENTING TIME REASONABLY AVAIL-
8 ABLE, THE COURT MAY DENY PARENTING TIME.
9   (4) A temporary restraining order to prevent domestic abuse may be
10 issued only if the issuing judge finds that an imminent danger exists to
11 the life or health of one or more persons; HOWEVER, THE COURT
12 SHALL NOT DENY A PETITIONER THE RELIEF REQUESTED SOLELY
13 BECAUSE OF A LAPSE IN TIME BETWEEN AN ACT OF DOMESTIC
14 ABUSE AND THE FILING OF THE PETITION FOR A RESTRAINING
15 ORDER TO PREVENT DOMESTIC ABUSE.
16   (6) A copy of the complaint together with a copy of the temporary
17 restraining order to prevent domestic abuse and a copy of the citation
18 shall be served upon the defendant in accordance with the rules for the
19 service of process as provided in rule 304 of the Colorado rules of
20 county court civil procedure or rule 4 of the Colorado rules of civil
21 procedure BY DELIVERING COPIES THEREOF TO SUCH DEFENDANT
22 PERSONALLY, and the citation shall inform the defendant that, if the
23 defendant fails to appear in court in accordance with the terms of the
24 citation, THE TEMPORARY RESTRAINING ORDER TO PREVENT DO-
25 MESTIC ABUSE PREVIOUSLY ENTERED BY THE COURT SHALL BE
26 MADE PERMANENT WITHOUT FURTHER NOTICE OR SERVICE UPON
27 THE DEFENDANT. THE COURT MAY ALSO ISSUE a bench warrant
28 may be issued for the arrest of the defendant, IF THE DEFENDANT
29 FAILS TO APPEAR IN COURT IN ACCORDANCE WITH THE TERMS OF
30 THE CITATION.
31   (7.5) (a) Any person against whom a temporary restraining order is
32 issued pursuant to this section, which temporary restraining order
33 excludes such person from a shared residence, shall be permitted to
34 return to such shared residence one time to obtain sufficient undis-
35 puted personal effects as are necessary for such person to maintain a
36 normal standard of living during any period prior to a hearing con-
37 cerning such order. Such person against whom a temporary restrain-

1 ing order is issued shall be permitted to return to such shared
2 residence only if such person is accompanied at all times while the
3 person is at or in such shared residence by a police officer.
4   **SECTION 4. 14-4-104 (1),** 1987 Repl. Vol., as amended, is
5 amended to read:
6   **14–4–104. Duties of peace officers - enforcement of restraining**
7 **orders and emergency protection orders.** (1) (a) A peace officer
8 shall use every reasonable means to enforce a restraining order
9 issued by a district or county court. Whenever there is exhibited to
10 any duly authorized sheriff or police officer an emergency protection
11 order or certified copy of a restraining order issued by any district or
12 county court, OR SUCH SHERIFF OR OFFICER VERIFIES BY MEANS
13 OF A CRIME INFORMATION CENTER THAT A RESTRAINING ORDER
14 OR EMERGENCY PROTECTION ORDER IS IN EFFECT, restraining
15 and enjoining any person from threatening, molesting, injuring, or
16 contacting any other person, or requiring the person to remove
17 himself OR HERSELF from certain premises and to refrain from
18 entering or remaining near or upon the premises thereafter, and when-
19 ever the copy of the emergency protection order or restraining order
20 shows, under signature of the person so serving, that a copy of the
21 order has been properly served upon the person named in the notice of
22 the existence and substance of such order, and whenever the sheriff or
23 police officer has probable cause to believe that the alleged violator has
24 been threatening, molesting, or injuring any person, or entering or
25 remaining on the premises in violation of the order, OR CONTACTING A
26 PERSON PROTECTED AGAINST SUCH CONTACT BY A RESTRAINING
27 ORDER, it is the duty of the sheriff or police officer to arrest the alleged
28 violator FOR THE VIOLATION OF A RESTRAINING ORDER and take
29 ~~him~~ THE ALLEGED VIOLATOR immediately ~~before the court issuing the~~
30 ~~emergency protection order or restraining order or, if that court is not in~~
31 ~~session,~~ to the nearest jail. ~~until the convening of the next session of the~~
32 ~~court, but in no event to exceed seventy-two hours unless extended for~~
33 ~~good cause shown by the issuing court, to await further action for the~~
34 ~~violation.~~ A peace officer shall not be held civilly or criminally liable for
35 acting pursuant to this section if ~~he~~ THE PEACE OFFICER acts in good
36 faith and without malice.

1   **SECTION 5.** 16-3-402, 1986 Repl. Vol., as amended, is amended
2 BY THE ADDITION OF A NEW SUBSECTION to read:
3   **16-3-402. Right to communicate with attorney and family.** IF THE
4 VICTIM IS ABLE TO DEMONSTRATE THROUGH THE USE OF
5 CALLER I.D. OR OTHER CREDIBLE EVIDENCE THAT THE INCAR-
6 CERATED DEFENDANT HAS CALLED THE VICTIM FROM THE JAIL
7 OR CORRECTIONAL FACILITY IN VIOLATION OF THE RESTRAINING
8 ORDER ISSUED PURSUANT TO SECTION 18-1-1001, OR IN VIOLA-
9 TION OF ANY OTHER VALID RESTRAINING ORDER OR EMER-
10 GENCY PROTECTION ORDER IN EFFECT, THEN THE DEFENDANT
11 SHALL NOT BE ENTITLED TO FURTHER TELEPHONE CALLS
12 EXCEPT TO SUCH DEFENDANT'S ATTORNEY, WHICH CALLS SHALL
13 BE PLACED BY A JAIL OR CORRECTIONAL FACILITY STAFF MEM-
14 BER. IF THE DEFENDANT WAS ARRESTED FOR VIOLATING AN
15 ORDER NOT TO CONTACT CERTAIN FAMILY MEMBERS, THE RIGHT
16 TO CONTACT THOSE FAMILY MEMBERS BY TELEPHONE SHALL BE
17 PROHIBITED, AND THE JAIL OR CORRECTIONAL FACILITY STAFF
18 SHALL PLACE ALL OUTGOING TELEPHONE CALLS THAT THE
19 DEFENDANT WISHES TO MAKE WHICH ARE NOT IDENTIFIED IN THE
20 RESTRAINING ORDER AS PROHIBITED.
21   **SECTION 6. Effective date - applicability.** This act shall take effect
22 July 1, 1994, and shall apply to orders entered on or after said date.

House Bill 107

Representative Lyle Spahnser's bill to require motorcyclists to wear helmets went to the Transportation committee. The committee chair, Representative Casey Anderson, recognized Representative Spahnser.

"Mr. Chairman, members of the committee," Representative Spahnser said, "this proposal is one that we have considered before. It simply requires motorcyclists, in the interest of safety, to wear helmets. As I'm sure you know, Congress passed legislation requiring the individual states to enact a mandatory helmet law or lose a portion of the state's federal funds for highways. If we do not pass this legislation, our State Highway Department will have $5 million less for highway construction. I hope that you will report this bill out, both in the interest of safety and in the interest of improving the highways in our state."

"Are there questions from the committee?" Representative Anderson asked. "The chair recognizes Representative Klein."

"Representative Spahnser," Klein said, "do I understand correctly that the U.S. Congress is telling us that we must pass legislation requiring motorcyclists to wear helmets, and that if we do not, the state will still receive $5 million in federal funds, but that money cannot be used for highway construction?"

"That's correct, Representative Klein. The $5 million in federal money would have to be used for safety programs. None of it, not a dime, could be used for highway construction."

"That's what I thought," Klein continued. "But I have heard that Congress is considering legislation that would eliminate the requirement that states enact a helmet law or lose federal funds for highway construction."

"You are correct again, Representative Klein. But we cannot be certain that Congress will pass the legislation you're talking about. And whether Congress does, or does not, pass the legislation you mentioned, I submit that this bill deserves your support," Representative Spahnser argued, "because of the safety issue alone. It would result in saving some lives and preventing serious injuries."

"Are there other questions from the committee?" Representative Anderson asked. "The chair recognizes Representative Kogovsek."

"I don't have any questions," Kogovsek stated, "but I want to say that I'm going to vote against this bill. In the first place, I think it is very likely that Congress will pass the legislation Representative Klein mentioned. And in the second place, I think government has no business telling individuals they have to wear a helmet if they're going to ride a motorcycle.

"So I'm going to vote against this bill, and I hope that a majority of the members of this committee will join me."

A majority of the committee members did join Representative Kogovsek in voting against the bill, which was killed on a 10-2 vote.

First Regular Session
Fifty-ninth General Assembly

STATE OF	HOUSE BILL 107
BY REPRESENTATIVE Spahnser	TRANSPORTATION

A BILL FOR AN ACT
CONCERNING MOTORIZED VEHICLES WITH THREE OR FEWER WHEELS,

AND,

IN CONNECTION THEREWITH, REQUIRING RIDERS ON MOTORCYCLES
AND MOTORIZED BICYCLES TO WEAR PROTECTIVE HELMETS

Bill Summary

(Note: This summary applies to this bill as introduced and does not necessarily reflect any amendments which may be subsequently adopted.)

Requires operators and passengers on motorcycles and motorized bicycles to wear protective helmets. Requires that helmets meet certain requirements, including standards adopted by the United States department of transportation. Authorizes issuance of permits exempting persons participating in parades or other public exhibitions.

Eliminates the exemption from personal injury protection insurance requirements allowed for motorcycle owners.

Presumes that any individual who rides a motorcycle without protective helmet waives the right to collect any damages for injuries suffered in a traffic accident that would have been reduced or eliminated if a protective helmet had been worn.

Capital letters indicate new material to be added to existing statute.

Dashes through the words indicate deletions from existing statute.

1 *Be it enacted by the General Assembly of the State:*

2   **SECTION 1.** 42-4-231 (2) is RECREATED AND REENACTED, WITH

3 AMENDMENTS, to read:

4   **42-4-231. Minimum safety standards for motorcycles and motor-**

5 **driven cycles - helmet requirement for motorcycles and motorized**

6 **bicycles.** (2) (a) A PERSON MAY NOT OPERATE ANY MOTORCYCLE OR

7 MOTORIZED BICYCLE ON ANY HIGHWAY IN THIS STATE UNLESS THE

8 OPERATOR AND ANY PASSENGER RIDING THE MOTORCYCLE OR

9 MOTORIZED BICYCLE ARE WEARING, SECURELY FASTENED ON EACH

10 PERSON'S HEAD, A PROTECTIVE HELMET THAT:

11   (I) IS EQUIPPED TO DEFLECT BLOWS, RESIST PENETRATION,

12 AND SPREAD THE FORCE OF IMPACT;

13   (II) IS EQUIPPED WITH EITHER A NECK OR CHIN STRAP;

14   (III) IS COATED WITH A REFLECTORIZED SUBSTANCE OR HAS A

15 MINIMUM OF FOUR SQUARE INCHES OF REFLECTORIZED MATERIAL

16 ATTACHED ON EACH SIDE OF THE HELMET AND ON THE BACK OF

Capital letters indicate new material to be added to existing statute.

Dashes through the words indicate deletions from existing statute.

1 THE HELMET; AND

2 (IV) MEETS OR EXCEEDS THE STANDARDS ESTABLISHED IN THE
3 UNITED STATES DEPARTMENT OF TRANSPORTATION'S FEDERAL MO-
4 TOR VEHICLE SAFETY STANDARD NO. 218, 49 C.F.R. 571.218, FOR
5 MOTORCYCLE HELMETS.

6 (b) THE POLICE AUTHORITIES OF A MUNICIPALITY OR THE SHER-
7 IFF OF A COUNTY MAY ISSUE A PERMIT TO MEMBERS OF AN ORGANI-
8 ZATION SPONSORING OR CONDUCTING A PARADE OR OTHER PUB-
9 LIC EXHIBITION EXEMPTING THE MEMBERS FROM THE PROVISIONS
10 OF THIS SUBSECTION (2) DURING THE PARADE OR PUBLIC EXHIBI-
11 TION.

12 **SECTION 2.** 10-4-703 (7), is amended to read:

13 **10-4-703. Definitions.** As used in this part 7, unless the context
14 otherwise requires:

15 (7) "Motor vehicle" means any vehicle of a type required to be
16 registered and licensed under the laws of this state and which is de-
17 signed to be propelled by an engine or motor; except that this term does
18 not include minibikes, snowmobiles, bicycles with motor or engine at-
19 tached, or any vehicle designed primarily for use off the road or on rails.

20 **SECTION 3.** 10-4-705 (3). Is repealed as follows:
21 **10-4-705. Coverage compulsory.** (3) For the purpose of subsection (1)
22 of this section, the definition of "motor vehicle" also includes "motor-
23 cycle" and "motorscooter", as such terms are defined in section 42-1-
24 102; except that the complying policy shall be limited to the coverage
25 required by section 10-4-706 (1) (a).

26 **SECTION 4.** Part 1 of article 21 of title 13, as amended, is amended
27 BY THE ADDITION OF A NEW SECTION to read:

28 **13-21-121. Liability for accidents involving motorcycles or mo-**
29 **torized bicycles - failure to wear protective helmet - assumption of**
30 **risk.** (1) FOR THE PURPOSES OF THIS SECTION, UNLESS THE CON-
31 TEXT OTHERWISE REQUIRES:

32 (a) "HIGHWAY" HAS THE MEANING PROVIDED FOR THE TERM IN
33 SECTION 42-1-1-2 (33),

34 (b) "MOTORCYCLE" HAS THE MEANING PROVIDED FOR THE TERM
35 IN SECTION 42-1-1-2 (44),

36 (c) "MOTORIZED BICYCLE" HAS THE MEANING PROVIDED FOR
37 THE TERM IN SECTION 42-1-102 (47) (b),

76

1   (d) "TRAFFIC ACCIDENT" MEANS ANY INCIDENT ON A HIGHWAY
2 IN WHICH A PERSONAL INJURY RESULTS FROM A COLLISION OR
3 OTHER ACCIDENT INVOLVING ONE OR MORE MOTOR VEHICLES.
4   (2) (a) IF ANY INDIVIDUAL RIDING ON A MOTORCYCLE OR MO-
5 TORIZED BICYCLE HAS AN OPERATOR OR PASSENGER INJURED IN A
6 TRAFFIC ACCIDENT AND THE INDIVIDUAL HAS FAILED TO WEAR A
7 PROTECTIVE HELMET IN VIOLATION OF SECTION 42-4-231 (2), THE
8 INDIVIDUAL IS PRESUMED TO HAVE ASSUMED THE RISK OF ANY IN-
9 JURY THAT WOULD HAVE BEEN PREVENTED OR REDUCED IF THE
10 INDIVIDUAL HAD WORN A PROTECTIVE HELMET IN ACCORDANCE
11 WITH SECTION 42-4-231 (2),
12   (b) EXCEPT AS PROVIDED IN SUBSECTION (3) OF THIS SECTION,
13 A PERSON INVOLVED IN OR RESPONSIBLE FOR A TRAFFIC ACCIDENT
14 WITH A MOTORCYCLE OR MOTORIZED BICYCLE IS NOT LIABLE FOR
15 ANY INJURY TO AN INDIVIDUAL RIDING ON THE MOTORCYCLE OR
16 MOTORIZED BICYCLE AS AN OPERATOR OR PASSENGER THAT RE-
17 SULTED FROM THE TRAFFIC ACCIDENT IF THE INDIVIDUAL WAS NOT
18 WEARING A PROTECTIVE HELMET AS REQUIRED BY SECTION 42-4-
19 231 (2), AND IF THE INJURY WOULD HAVE BEEN PREVENTED OR
20 REDUCED IF THE INDIVIDUAL HAD BEEN WEARING A PROTECTIVE
21 HELMET. A PERSON RIDING A MOTORCYCLE OR MOTORIZED BI-
22 CYCLE WHO IS INJURED IN A TRAFFIC ACCIDENT OR A REPRESENTA-
23 TIVE OR SUCH PERSON MAY NOT MAKE ANY CLAIM AGAINST, MAIN-
24 TAIN AN ACTION AGAINST, OR RECOVER FROM ANY PERSON IN-
25 VOLVED IN OR RESPONSIBLE FOR THE TRAFFIC ACCIDENT IF THE
26 INDIVIDUAL WAS NOT WEARING A PROTECTIVE HELMET AS REQUIRED
27 BY SECTION 42-4-231 (2) AND IF THE INJURY SUFFERED BY THE
28 INDIVIDUAL WOULD HAVE BEEN PREVENTED OR REDUCED IF THE
29 INDIVIDUAL HAD BEEN WEARING A PROTECTIVE HELMET.
30   (3) NOTHING IN THIS SECTION PREVENTS OR LIMITS THE LIABIL-
31 ITY OF A PERSON INVOLVED IN OR RESPONSIBLE FOR A TRAFFIC
32 ACCIDENT INVOLVING A MOTORCYCLE OR MOTORIZED BICYCLE IF
33 THE PERSON INTENTIONALLY INJURES ANY INDIVIDUAL WHO IS
34 RIDING A MOTORCYCLE OR MOTORIZED BICYCLE.
35   **SECTION 5. Effective date - applicability.** This act shall take effect
36   July 1, 1994, and shall apply to offenses committed and incidents
37   occurring on or after said date.

```
1      SECTION 6. Safety clause. The general assembly hereby finds,
2   determines, and declares that this act is necessary for the immediate
3   preservation of the public peace, health, and safety.
```

House Bill 20

Representative Spahnser's second bill was referred to the State Affairs committee.

"The intent of this bill," he told the committee, "is to address what has become a major concern of many of our constituents—violent street gangs whose members threaten, terrorize, and commit crimes against peaceful citizens.

"To get at the problem, this bill creates penalties for a new offense: active participation in a criminal street gang.

"Criminal street gang is defined as 'any ongoing organization, association, or group of three or more persons, whether formal or informal, which carries on as one of its primary activities the commission of one or more of the criminal acts prohibited by state statutes, which has a common name or common identifying sign or symbol, and the members of which individually or collectively engage in or have engaged in a pattern of criminal gang activity.'

"Admittedly, that's a lengthy definition," Representative Spahnser said, "but I think it is necessary in this instance. It was also necessary to include a lengthy definition of another new term 'pattern of criminal gang activity.' It is on page 3 of the bill, beginning with line 13.

"Another thing we've attempted to do with this bill is to put some responsibility on the parents of juveniles by making them subject to penalties if they recklessly disregard a juvenile's participation in a criminal street gang.

"Mr. Chairman and members of the committee, I apologize for this rather lengthy explanation, but I believe this legislation could be an important tool in making our streets safe for ordinary citizens, something we all want to do."

The committee members had numerous questions concerning the details of the bill, especially the definitions of the new offenses and legal challenges that might be based on the constitutionally protected rights of freedom of expression and association.

After considerable discussion centered on legal problems with the bill, plus concerns about the difficulty of enforcing its provisions, the committee voted to kill the bill.

HOUSE BILL 20

STATE OF

BY REPRESENTATIVE Spahnser

STATE AFFAIRS

A BILL FOR AN ACT

CONCERNING THE PREVENTION OF CRIMINAL ACTIVITY, AND, IN CON-
NECTION THEREWITH, ENACTING MEASURES TO PREVENT JUVENILE
AND GANG-RELATED CRIMES.

Bill Summary

**(Note: This summary applies to this bill as introduced and does not
necessarily reflect any amendments which may be subsequently
adopted.)**

Creates the offense of active participation in a criminal street gang and
provides a penalty therefor. Establishes that a parent or legal guardian shall
be deemed to have committed such offense if such parent or legal guardian
recklessly disregards a juvenile's participation in a criminal street gang.
Defines "criminal street gang" and "pattern of criminal gang activity." Provides for enhanced sentences for misdemeanors committed for the benefit
of, at the direction of, or in association with any criminal street gang. Makes
any property used in furtherance of a pattern of criminal gang activity by a
criminal street gang a class 1 public nuisance.

Establishes the following as factors to be considered by the juvenile
court in determining whether to waive juvenile court jurisdiction over a
juvenile for the commission of a delinquent act and transfer the case to the
district court: Whether the juvenile used or possessed and threatened to use
a deadly weapon in the commission of the delinquent act; and whether the
juvenile was a member of a gang and the delinquent act was committed in
furtherance of gang membership.

1   *Be it enacted by the General Assembly of the State :*
2   **SECTION 1**. Part 1 of article 9 of title 18, Revised Statutes, 1986
3   Repl. Vol., as amended, is amended BY THE ADDITION OF A NEW

1 SECTION to read:

2 **18-9-123. Active participation in criminal street gang - misde-**
3 **meanor - penalty - legislative declaration - definitions**. (1) THE GEN-
4 ERAL ASSEMBLY HEREBY FINDS AND DECLARES THAT IT IS THE
5 RIGHT OF EVERY PERSON TO BE SECURE AND PROTECTED FROM
6 FEAR, INTIMIDATION, AND PHYSICAL HARM CAUSED BY THE ACTIVI-
7 TIES OF VIOLENT GROUPS AND INDIVIDUALS. IT IS NOT THE INTENT
8 OF THIS SECTION TO INTERFERE WITH THE EXERCISE OF THE CON-
9 STITUTIONALLY PROTECTED RIGHTS OF FREEDOM OF EXPRESSION
10 AND ASSOCIATION. THE GENERAL ASSEMBLY HEREBY RECOGNIZES
11 THE CONSTITUTIONAL RIGHT OF EVERY CITIZEN TO HARBOR AND
12 EXPRESS BELIEFS ON ANY LAWFUL SUBJECT WHATSOEVER, TO
13 LAWFULLY ASSOCIATE WITH OTHERS WHO SHARE SIMILAR BELIEFS,
14 TO PETITION LAWFULLY CONSTITUTED AUTHORITY FOR A REDRESS
15 OF PERCEIVED GRIEVANCES, AND TO PARTICIPATE IN THE ELEC-
16 TORAL PROCESS. HOWEVER, THE GENERAL ASSEMBLY FURTHER
17 FINDS THAT THE STATE IS IN A STATE OF CRISIS WHICH HAS BEEN
18 CAUSED BY VIOLENT STREET GANGS WHOSE MEMBERS THREATEN,
19 TERRORIZE, AND COMMIT A MULTITUDE OF CRIMES AGAINST THE
20 PEACEFUL CITIZENS OF THIS STATE AND INVOLVE OR RECRUIT
21 JUVENILES TO ENGAGE IN VIOLENT CRIMINAL ACTIVITY. THE ACTIVI-
22 TIES OF SUCH VIOLENT STREET GANGS PRESENT A CLEAR AND
23 PRESENT DANGER TO PUBLIC ORDER AND SAFETY AND ARE NOT
24 CONSTITUTIONALLY PROTECTED. IT IS THE INTENT OF THE GEN-
25 ERAL ASSEMBLY IN ENACTING THIS SECTION TO SEEK THE ERADI-
26 CATION OF CRIMINAL ACTIVITY BY STREET GANGS BY FOCUSING
27 UPON PATTERNS OF CRIMINAL GANG ACTIVITY AND UPON THE OR-
28 GANIZED NATURE OF STREET GANGS.

29 (2) ANY PERSON WHO ACTIVELY PARTICIPATES IN ANY CRIMI-
30 NAL STREET GANG WITH KNOWLEDGE THAT THE MEMBERS OF
31 SUCH CRIMINAL STREET GANG ENGAGE IN OR HAVE ENGAGED IN
32 A PATTERN OF CRIMINAL GANG ACTIVITY, OR WHO WILLFULLY
33 PROMOTES, FURTHERS, OR ASSISTS IN ANY CRIMINAL CONDUCT
34 PROHIBITED PURSUANT TO THE STATUTES OF THE STATE BY
35 MEMBERS OF SUCH CRIMINAL STREET GANG, COMMITS THE

Capital letters indicate new material to be added to existing statute.
Dashes through the words indicate deletions from existing statute.

1 OFFENSE OF ACTIVE PARTICIPATION IN A CRIMINAL STREET GANG.

2 (3) ACTIVE PARTICIPATION IN A CRIMINAL STREET GANG IS A

3 CLASS 1 MISDEMEANOR.

4 (4) AS USED IN THIS SECTION AND SECTION 18-9-124:

5 (a) "CRIMINAL STREET GANG" MEANS ANY ONGOING ORGANIZA-

6 TION, ASSOCIATION, OR GROUP OF THREE OR MORE PERSONS,

7 WHETHER FORMAL OR INFORMAL, WHICH CARRIES ON AS ONE OF

8 ITS PRIMARY ACTIVITIES THE COMMISSION OF ONE OR MORE OF

9 THE CRIMINAL ACTS PROHIBITED BY THE STATUTES WHICH HAS A

10 COMMON NAME OR COMMON IDENTIFYING SIGN OR SYMBOL, AND

11 THE MEMBERS OF WHICH INDIVIDUALLY OR COLLECTIVELY ENGAGE

12 IN OR HAVE ENGAGED IN A PATTERN OF CRIMINAL GANG ACTIVITY.

13 (b) "PATTERN OF CRIMINAL GANG ACTIVITY" MEANS THE COM-

14 MISSION, ATTEMPTED COMMISSION, CONSPIRACY TO COMMIT, OR

15 SOLICITATION TO COMMIT TWO OR MORE CRIMINAL OFFENSES

16 PROHIBITED PURSUANT TO THE STATUTES IF AT LEAST ONE OF

17 SUCH OFFENSES, OR THE ATTEMPT, CONSPIRACY, OR SOLICITA-

18 TION OF SUCH OFFENSES, OCCURRED SUBSEQUENT TO THE EF-

19 FECTIVE DATE OF THIS SECTION, AND THE LAST OF SUCH OF-

20 FENSES, OR THE ATTEMPT, CONSPIRACY, OR SOLICITATION OF SUCH

21 OFFENSES, OCCURRED WITHIN THREE YEARS AFTER THE FIRST OF

22 SUCH OFFENSES, AND ALL OF THE OFFENSES ALLEGED TO BE A

23 PART OF SUCH ACTIVITY, OR THE ATTEMPT, CONSPIRACY, OR SO-

24 LICITATION OF SUCH OFFENSES, OCCURRED ON SEPARATE OCCA-

25 SIONS.

26 (5) (a) FOR PURPOSES OF THIS SECTION, A PARENT OR LEGAL

27 GUARDIAN OF ANY JUVENILE, AS DEFINED IN SECTION 19-2-102 (7),

28 WHO IS RESIDING WITH SUCH PARENT OR GUARDIAN SHALL HAVE

29 THE DUTY TO EXERCISE REASONABLE CARE, SUPERVISION, PRO-

30 TECTION, AND CONTROL OVER SUCH JUVENILE TO PREVENT OR

31 CURTAIL SUCH JUVENILE FROM PARTICIPATING IN ANY CRIMINAL

32 STREET GANG.

33 (b) THE PARENT OR LEGAL GUARDIAN OF ANY JUVENILE DE-

34 SCRIBED IN PARAGRAPH (a) OF THIS SUBSECTION (5) COMMITS A

35 CLASS 1 MISDEMEANOR IF SUCH PARENT OR LEGAL GUARDIAN

36 RECKLESSLY DISREGARDS SUCH JUVENILE'S PARTICIPATION IN ANY

37 CRIMINAL STREET GANG AND FAILS TO MAKE REASONABLE EF-

1 FORTS TO PREVENT OR CURTAIL SUCH JUVENILE'S PARTICIPATION
2 IN ANY CRIMINAL STREET GANG.
3   (c) ANY PARENT OR LEGAL GUARDIAN OF ANY JUVENILE DE-
4 SCRIBED IN PARAGRAPH (a) OF THIS SUBSECTION (5) WHO IS CON-
5 VICTED OF A VIOLATION OF THIS SECTION MAY BE ORDERED BY THE
6 SENTENCING COURT, IN ADDITION TO THE PENALTY PROVIDED BY
7 PARAGRAPH (b) OF THIS SUBSECTION (5), TO ATTEND A PARENTAL
8 RESPONSIBILITY TRAINING PROGRAM AS DIRECTED BY THE COURT.
9   **SECTION 2**. 18-1-106 (3), Revised Statutes, 1986 Repl. Vol., as
10 amended, is amended to read:
11   **18-1-106. Misdemeanors classified - penalties.**
12 (3) (a) The general assembly hereby finds that certain misdemeanors
13 which are listed in paragraph (b) of this subsection (3) present an
14 extraordinary risk of harm to society and therefore, in the interest of
15 public safety, the maximum sentence in the presumptive range for such
16 misdemeanors shall be increased by six months.
17   (b) Misdemeanors which present an extraordinary risk of harm to
18 society shall include the following:
19   (I)   Assault in the third degree, as defined in section 18-3-204;
20   (II) Sexual assault in the third degree, as defined in section 18-3-404;
21   (III)   Child abuse, as defined in section 18-6-401 (7) (a) (V): ~~and~~
22   (IV) Harassment by stalking, as defined in section 18-9-111 (4); and
23   (V) ANY MISDEMEANOR COMMITTED FOR THE BENEFIT OF, AT
24 THE DIRECTION OF, OR IN ASSOCIATION WITH ANY CRIMINAL STREET
25 GANG WITH THE SPECIFIC INTENT TO PROMOTE, FURTHER, OR
26 ASSIST IN ANY PATTERN OF CRIMINAL GANG ACTIVITY BY ANY CRIMI-
27 NAL STREET GANG, AS DESCRIBED IN SECTION 18-9-123.
28   **SECTION 3**. 16-13-303 (1) (I), Revised Statutes, 1986 Repl. Vol., as
29 amended, is amended to read:
30   **16-13-303. Class 1 public nuisance**. (1) Every building or part of a
31 building including the ground upon which it is situate and all fixtures and
32 contents thereof, every vehicle, and any real property shall be deemed a
33 class 1 public nuisance when:
34   (1) Used in committing a drive-by crime, as defined in section 16-13-
35 301 (2.2), OR IN FURTHERANCE OF ANY PATTERN OF CRIMINAL GANG
36 ACTIVITY, AS DEFINED IN SECTION 18-9-123 (4) (b),
37 BY ANY CRIMINAL STREET GANG, AS DEFINED IN SECTION 18-9-123
38 (4) (a),

1   **SECTION 4**. 19-2-806 (3) (b), Revised Statutes, 1986-Repl. Vol., as
2   amended, is amended to read:

3   **19-2-806. Transfer proceedings**. (3) (b) In considering whether or
4   not to waive juvenile court jurisdiction over the juvenile, the juvenile court
5   shall consider the following factors:

6   (I) The seriousness of the offense and whether the protection of the
7   community requires isolation of the juvenile beyond that afforded by
8   juvenile facilities;

9   (II) Whether the alleged offense was committed in an aggressive,
10   violent, premeditated, or willful manner;

11   (III) Whether the alleged offense was against persons or property,
12   greater weight being given to offenses against persons;

13   (IV) The maturity of the juvenile as determined by considerations of
14   ~~his~~ THE JUVENILE'S home, environment, emotional attitude, and pattern
15   of living;

16   (V) The record and previous history of the juvenile;

17   (VI) The likelihood of rehabilitation of the juvenile by use of facilities
18   available to the juvenile court;

19   (VII) The interest of the community in the imposition of a punishment
20   commensurate with the gravity of the offense;

21   (VIII) The impact of the offense on the victim;

22   (IX) That the juvenile was previously adjudicated a juvenile delin-
23   quent for a delinquent act which constitutes a crime of violence, as
24   defined in section 16-11-309.

25   (X) That the juvenile was previously committed to the department of
26   institutions following an adjudication for a delinquent act which consti-
27   tutes a felony;

28   (XI) That the juvenile is sixteen years of age or older at the time of
29   the offense and present act constitutes a crime of violence, as defined in
30   section 16-11-309, ~~and~~

31   (XII) That the juvenile is sixteen years of age or older at the time of
32   the offense and has been twice previously adjudicated a juvenile delin-
33   quent for delinquent acts against property which constitute felonies;

34   (XIII) THE USE OF, OR THE POSSESSION AND THREATENED USE
35   OF, A DEADLY WEAPON IN THE COMMISSION OF A DELINQUENT ACT;
36   AND

37   (XIV) THAT AT THE TIME OF THE COMMISSION OF A DELINQUENT
38   ACT THE JUVENILE WAS A MEMBER OF A "GANG," AS DEFINED IN

```
1    SECTION 19-2-204 (4) (e) (II), AND SUCH DELINQUENT ACT WAS
2    COMMITTED IN FURTHERANCE OF SUCH GANG MEMBERSHIP.
3        SECTION 5. Effective date - applicability. This act shall take effect
4    upon passage and shall apply to offenses committed on or after said
5    date.
6        SECTION 6. Safety clause. The general assembly hereby finds,
7    determines, and declares that this act is necessary for the immediate
8    preservation of the public peace, health, and safety.
```

SUMMARY

Committees are the heart of the legislative process, the place where much of a legislature's work takes place. It is during committee consideration that individual citizens have the best opportunity to express their views on pending legislation, and it is during committee consideration that legislators have their best opportunity to work over bills thoroughly.

Standing committees play the major role, but several other types—select, interim, and joint committees—also have input in the legislative process.

Even though no two state legislatures operate in precisely the same way, many state legislative committees have similar options for acting on legislation, including a vote to report a bill with a recommendation to pass, to fail, or with no recommendation, or a vote to kill a bill—which happens to a majority of bills referred to committee.

TABLE 6.1

OPTIONS AVAILABLE TO STANDING COMMITTEES FOR DISPOSING OF BILLS

State	Recommend to Pass	Recommend to Pass With Amendments	Report Without Recommendation	Give an Adverse Report	Postpone the Bill Indefinitely	Kill the Bill in Committee	Other
Alabama	B	B	S	S	B	B	S-do nothing
Alaska	B	B	B	B	B	B	
Arizona	B	B	S		H	S	H-do not pass; return for consideration of House
Arkansas	B	B		B		S	
California	H	H	H	H	H	H	H-refer bill to interim study
Colorado	B	B	H		B	B	H-refer bill to another committee
Connecticut	B	B	B	B	B	B	B-refer bill to another committee
Delaware	B	H	B	B	S	H	
Florida	B	B		H		S	H-refer to subcmte; favorable rpt w/cmte substitute
Georgia	B	B	H	B		H	
Hawaii	B	B			H	S	
Idaho	S	S	S		S	S	
Illinois	B	B	S	H	B	H	
Indiana	B	B	B		B	B	
Iowa	B	B	B	S	S	B	
Kansas	B	B	B	B	S	B	
Kentucky	B	B	B	B	B	B	S-recommend bill be referred to another cmte
Louisiana	B	B	B	B	B	B	S-new draft; H-report in a divided report
Maine	B	B		B	B	B	B-refer to an interim study
Maryland	B	B	B	B			
Massachusetts	B	B			H	H	S-report bill with changes; H-place bill into study
Michigan	B	B	B		B	B	S-recommend bill be referred to another cmte
Minnesota	B	B	B		B	B	
Mississippi	B	B		B	S	B	
Missouri	B	B	B	B		H	B-table the bill in committee
Montana	B	B		B	H		
Nebraska	S	S			S	S	
Nevada	B	B	B	B	B	B	B-refer to cmte; place on consent calendar

TABLE 6.1 (CONTINUED)

OPTIONS AVAILABLE TO STANDING COMMITTEES FOR DISPOSING OF BILLS

State	Recommend to Pass	Recommend to Pass With Amendments	Report Without Recommendation	Give an Adverse Report	Postpone the Bill Indefinitely	Kill the Bill in Committee	Other
New Hampshire	B	B	B	B			B-interim study; refer bill to next session
New Jersey	B	B	B	S	B	S	H-report a committee substitute
New Mexico	B	B	B	B	B	B	S-remove from committee to calendar
New York	H	H	S	H	H	S	
North Carolina	B	B		B	H	B	S-withdraw for previously ordered sequential referral
North Dakota	B	B		B	H	B	B-refer to another cmte; rpt it be defeated as amended
Ohio	B	B	S			B	H-refer bill to another committee
Oklahoma	B	B		H	B	B	
Oregon	B	B	B	B	B	B	B-refer to another committee; table the bill
Pennsylvania	B	B	S	B	B	B	
Rhode Island	*						
South Carolina	H	H				H	
South Dakota	B	B	B	B	B	B	B-refer bill to another committee
Tennessee	B	B	H	H	H	B	
Texas	B	B	H	B	S	S	S-report committee substitute
Utah	B	B		S			
Vermont	B	B	B	B	B	S	S-table the bill in committee
Virginia	H	H			B	B	S-rpt bill; rpt bill w/amends; rpt substitute; do nothing
Washington	B	B	B	S	S		B-do nothing; S-report substitute bill
West Virginia	B	B	B	B	B	B	
Wisconsin	B	B	B	B		B	
Wyoming	B	B	B		B	B	

Key:
B = Both chambers
S = Senate or Council only
H = House or Assembly only
* = Did not respond to survey

CHAPTER

On the Floor

Bills that have been reported from committee are scheduled for debate on the floor by the full membership, followed, finally, by a vote on passage of the legislation. In the following chapter we will be looking at the way most state legislative chambers proceed with consideration of bills by the full membership. Our legislators, Senator Brian Caucus and Representatives Margaret Justice and Lyle Spahnser, introduced six bills that we followed through the committee process. Three of their bills were killed in committee; three were reported favorably by the standing committees to which they were assigned at introduction. We will be following these three bills through their consideration by the full membership.

In legislative language "the floor" refers to the chambers of the House and Senate and to a specific step in the legislative process. When a bill is reported from committee, it is ready to go "to the floor" for action by the full membership of the House or Senate. Bills do not move directly to the floor, however. A committee's action must be reported to the House or Senate at a daily session and scheduled for consideration by being placed on the chamber's calendar. The time between committee action on a bill and its consideration by the full membership varies. In some states the scheduling of bills is determined by the order in which committee reports are received; in others, bills are scheduled for floor action by a **Rules** committee, a Calendar committee, or a similar panel responsible for

controlling the flow of legislation to the floor. Most bills that are reported
by committees are placed on the calendar, but in some legislatures every
bill may not be scheduled for consideration.

Legislative bodies follow an established order of business for their daily
sessions. There are variations in every legislature, of course, but a typical
order of business for a House chamber might look like this:

- Call of the roll. At the beginning of the session, the roll of
  members is called to determine who is present, and whether
  there is a **quorum**, which is necessary to conduct the business
  of the chamber.
- Introduction, first reading and reference of bills. This is the
  time when bills are formally introduced. The reading clerk
  reads the bill number, the sponsor, the title of the bill, and the
  committee, or committees, to which the bill is assigned.
- Reports of committees. The committee chairs report action
  taken by their respective committees on bills that were referred
  to them for consideration. Bills reported by a committee might
  be placed on the calendar for future consideration by the House
  or Senate, or might be referred to a Rules or Calendar committee.
- Messages from the Senate or House. Each chamber sends
  formal messages to the other body concerning action taken by
  the full membership, or other information regarding the business of the legislature. For example, the Senate might send a
  message to the House that it has passed, with amendments,
  House Bill 10—or the appropriate number.
- Consideration of conference committee reports. When conference committees have reached agreement on the differences
  between House and Senate versions of a bill, the conference
  committee reports its recommendations, and the House or
  Senate members decide whether to accept the conference
  committee's version. Action on a conference committee report
  does not have to occur immediately—it might be delayed to a
  future time.
- **Third reading** of House and Senate bills. Bills that are up for
  third reading—final passage—are those that were considered
  previously on second reading. On third reading, bills are acted
  upon—or **laid over** to another time or day—before a chamber
  takes up bills on the second reading calendar.

- **Second reading** of House and Senate bills. This is the time in the legislative process when bills are debated at length and amended, although bills may also be subject to amendment on third reading. On second reading, the House or Senate resolves itself into **Committee of the Whole**—that is, the full House or Senate becomes a committee for the purpose of debating and amending bills. When the second reading calendar for that day is completed, the Committee of the Whole must report its actions to the House or Senate.
- **Announcements.** This is the time reserved for various announcements of interest to the members, including, perhaps, changes in committee meeting schedules as well as other matters.
- **Adjournment.** When a legislative body has finished its agenda for the day, a motion for adjournment to a time and day is made and voted upon.

That is an abbreviated listing, but it is an illustration of the established order of business in many legislative chambers.

PARLIAMENTARY PROCEDURE

The operation of a legislature proceeds along prescribed lines, according to meticulous rules. Each legislative body makes its own rules; it does not necessarily follow, for example, *Roberts' Rules of Order*. In addition to the rules established by each chamber, the most frequently used references for legislative procedure are *Mason's Manual* and *Jefferson's Manual*. Legislative rules determine the way business is conducted on the floor. The rules—and in some instances, statutes or a state's constitution—provide for matters such as the order of business, the conduct of debate, the resolution of disputes, voting, and the precedence of motions.

Parliamentary procedure during floor consideration—particularly with regard to tactical maneuvers involving various motions—can be especially complicated. The most effective legislators are those who become thoroughly familiar with the rules of parliamentary procedure, a process that requires considerable study and experience. For that reason, we will discuss only a few procedures necessary for a basic understanding of the legislative process: readings, Committees of the Whole, limits on debate, and voting.

READINGS

With few exceptions, state legislative chambers require three readings of a bill. Nebraska's **unicameral** legislature requires four. Two readings are necessary in both the House and Senate in Maine, North Dakota, and South Dakota. The Iowa Senate requires two readings; the House three. "Reading" refers to various stages in the legislative process. It does not mean that the full text of bills are read each time they are considered—that rarely happens. First reading normally occurs when a bill is introduced by its title and assigned to a committee. Second reading, in most states, is when bills that have been reported from committee are brought to the floor for consideration. It is during second reading that all members have an opportunity to be heard and to offer amendments. Second reading is also the time when amendments that were adopted by a standing committee must be approved or rejected by the full membership. Third reading is the time when a vote is taken on final passage, usually without being subject to amendment unless **unanimous consent** is given. Again, there are exceptions in some states. In Alabama, for example, bills are debated, amended, and a vote is taken on final passage—all on third reading. Second reading in Alabama is merely the committee report.

Typically, readings must be on separate days—two or three days between readings in most states. Exceptions are the Senates in Iowa, Kentucky, New Jersey, New York, Virginia, and Washington; the Houses in Maine, Michigan, and Utah; and both chambers in New Hampshire.

COMMITTEE OF THE WHOLE

This is a parliamentary procedure that most legislative bodies utilize when bills are on second reading. The term means, literally, that the full membership of the House or Senate acts as a committee, operating in a similar fashion to standing committees. The major differences are that every legislator is a member of the committee and nonlegislators usually have no opportunity to be heard, as they do when standing committees hold hearings on a bill.

The Speaker of the House and the President of the Senate preside over the daily sessions of their chambers. When the chamber's regular order of business calls for second reading of bills, the chamber resolves itself into the Committee of the Whole, with a member designated by the Speaker or the Senate President to preside as chair. Any member may serve as chair of the Committee of the Whole. The bills eligible for consideration on second reading are listed on a calendar. They are taken up in the order in which they appear on the House or Senate calendar. Also, debate in Committee of the Whole is unlimited—that is, motions for the **previous question** or to end debate are not in order—roll-call votes are not taken, and a **call of the House** or Senate is not allowed. And since it is a committee, the Committee of the Whole must report its recommendations to the House or Senate.

As each bill comes up, the first person recognized to speak is the chair of the standing committee that considered the legislation and reported it.

If the bill was reported with amendments, the chair of the standing committee moves the adoption of the committee amendments and then explains the action taken during the committee's deliberations. Any member may speak to the question of approving or rejecting the amendments. Usually the first person recognized following the committee chair is the bill's sponsor. And after all the members have had an opportunity to speak to the committee amendments a vote is taken on their adoption—unless a motion has been made to reject them. In that event, the first vote would be on the question of rejecting the committee amendments. Assuming the motion failed, the vote would then be on their adoption.

If the amendments are adopted by the Committee of the Whole, the next step for the standing committee chair is to move adoption of the bill as amended. The same procedure would be followed on this question: the chair of the standing committee would be recognized first in order to explain why the committee reported the bill with a favorable recommendation, as amended. The sponsor would explain the bill further, answer questions, and give the members reasons why they should vote in favor of the legislation. Opponents would make their arguments and perhaps move that the bill not pass. If that motion were made, there would be a vote on the question that the bill not pass. Assuming the motion to reject the bill failed, the chair of the standing committee that reported the bill would move that it pass, as amended, on second reading. Since the previous motion that the bill not pass was voted down, it is obvious that the next motion—that the bill pass, as amended—would be successful. But a vote to pass the bill would still be necessary: it would not pass automatically because the motion to reject the bill was unsuccessful.

In general, the procedure we have outlined would be followed for each bill on the chamber's second reading calendar. When all bills on second reading had been considered, the majority floor leader would move that the committee—that is, the Committee of the Whole—**"rise and report."** The Speaker of the House or President of the Senate would then return to the chair as the **presiding officer,** and the member who had been acting as chair would report on the result of consideration of bills on second reading.

A formal vote on actions in the Committee of the Whole would then be taken. If those actions were approved, all the bills that were considered in Committee of the Whole—assuming they passed on second reading— would be placed on the calendar for third reading: final passage. If a bill passed on second reading during Committee of the Whole, it could be assumed that it would pass on third reading. In most cases, it would. But some members might change their vote between second and third reading, so that a positive vote on second reading does not automatically assure the passage of a bill on third reading—especially if the bill passed on second reading by a narrow margin.

LIMITS ON DEBATE

Time is a valuable commodity in the legislative process. If all the members of a legislative body were allowed unlimited time to speak during consideration of every bill, taking final action on all the legislation that reached the floor would consume more time than most legislatures can afford. That is especially true of House chambers, all of which have many more members than the Senate. An extreme example is New Hampshire where there are 400 members in the House and 24 in the Senate.

To allow a legislature to complete its business in a reasonable length of time, many legislatures—especially House chambers—limit debate. The most frequently used methods to accomplish this are restrictions on the number of times a member may speak on a question, generally once or twice, and time limits, which usually range from 5 to 15 minutes. There are 99 state legislative chambers and only 14 do not limit debate: the Senates in Alaska, Arizona, Iowa, Massachusetts, Minnesota, Missouri, Montana, Texas, and Virginia; the Houses in Delaware, Indiana, and Maryland; and both chambers in Connecticut.

There are also mechanisms for ending debate. The one allowed most frequently—in 82 chambers—is a motion, which can be made by any member, calling for the previous question. If the previous question were moved, a roll-call vote would be taken. If the motion passed, debate would end and a vote on the measure being considered would follow. A motion calling for the previous question is not allowed in Committee of the Whole. Other devices used by some legislatures include a motion to close debate at a certain time, a motion to close debate after a specific amount of time for discussion, and allocating time for debate on specific sections of the bill.

VOTING

There are several methods of voting. One is a simple **voice vote**. The chair calls for the members of a chamber or committee to vote by those in favor and those opposed, and then announces the result. Another is a **division vote**, usually taken by asking those in favor of a question to rise at their seats and repeating the process for those opposed. Voice and division votes are the most frequent methods of voting in Committee of the Whole. In both methods, there is no record of how individual members voted on a question.

Roll-call votes require a "yes" or "no" vote by each legislator, and the votes are recorded in the chamber's journal. A roll-call vote on final passage is mandatory in most states. Even in those where it is not, a member can demand a roll-call vote, and if supported by a certain number of members it must be taken.

In most state legislatures, the individual votes of members during consideration in Committee of the Whole are not recorded in the journal (the daily record of floor action). Thus a member's vote on key amendments and passage on second reading generally is not available to a constituent who might want to know how their representative or senator voted on a particular issue, nor is it available for political opponents who might want to use a member's voting record in the next election campaign. But since the passage or defeat of key amendments can have a significant effect on legislative proposals, there is a parliamentary maneuver, that enables members to force a roll-call vote on amendments that were considered during Committee of the Whole, and on passage or defeat of legislation at that point in the legislative process.

Suppose a member wanted to get all the members on record as to how they voted on a specific amendment that was rejected, or approved, during consideration in Committee of the Whole. When the Committee of the Whole has completed the agenda for that day's session, the Committee "rises and reports," which means that it reports, to the full membership of the House or Senate, action that was taken during consideration of legislation in Committee of the Whole. The House or Senate must then adopt the report of the Committee of the Whole.

Let's say, for example, that Representative Margaret Justice wanted to force a roll-call vote on an amendment (adopted on a voice vote in Committee of the Whole), to her gun control bill that stipulated that anyone under 18 can buy a rifle or shotgun if they receive instruction in firearms safety. That was the amendment, suggested by the National Rifle Association and sponsored by Representative Williams. The Williams

amendment passed on a voice vote in Committee of the Whole. Representative Justice's reason for wanting a **roll-call vote** would be to
get on record the names of members who supported the position of the
National Rifle Association. To do that she would offer an amendment to
the report of the Committee of the Whole to show that the Williams
amendment to House Bill 15 did not pass—essentially claiming that the
voice vote misrepresented the opinions of the Committee of the Whole.
Her amendment would force a roll-call vote, which would put all the
members of the House on record as to whether they did or did not support
the Williams amendment.

THREE BILLS ON THE FLOOR

We started out with six bills sponsored by Senator Brian Caucus and
Representatives Margaret Justice and Lyle Spahnser. Three were killed by
the standing committees to which they were assigned. The other three,
Senate Bills 21 and 155 by Senator Caucus, and House Bill 15 by Representative Justice were reported favorably from committee and have been
placed on second reading calendars in the Senate and House.

In the Senate

Senator Fred Trujillo, President of the Senate, rapped his gavel and called
the chamber to **order** Tuesday at 10 AM, the Senate's normal time to
convene for its daily session. He proceeded through the items on the
Senate's order of business to "Second Reading of Senate Bills." At that
point he recognized Senator Bob Jackson, who he had asked, before the
session started, to serve that day as chair of the Committee of the Whole.

"Mr. President," he said, "I move that the Senate resolve itself into
Committee of the Whole for consideration of Senate bills on second
reading."

"Without objection, so ordered," Senator Trujillo responded.

Senator Jackson took the chair and called the committee to order. The
first bill listed on the calendar was Senate Bill 21. Senator Jackson recognized Senator Doris Brooks, chair of the Local Government committee.

"Mr. Chairman," Senator Brooks said, "there is a **committee amendment** to Senate Bill 21."

"The clerk will read the amendment," Senator Jackson responded.

"Committee amendment to Senate Bill 21. On page 1, line 12, after the
word 'punishment' delete the word 'of' and substitute the word 'for.'"

"The chair recognizes Senator Brooks."

"I move the adoption of the committee amendment to Senate Bill 21," Senator Brooks said. "Mr. Chairman and members of the Senate, this is a very minor technical amendment to clarify the language of the bill," Senator Brooks explained. "If there are any questions I will be pleased to answer them. If there are none, I renew my motion for the adoption of the committee amendment."

The amendment was adopted on a voice vote.

"The chair recognizes Senator Caucus."

"Mr. Chairman, members of the Senate," Senator Caucus said, "I move the adoption of Senate Bill 21 on second reading, as amended. As I told members of the Local Government committee," he continued, "this is a simple, straightforward bill that gives the counties a tool to deal with some of the problems that may result from the actions of juveniles. It simply says that counties may adopt ordinances imposing curfews and regulating loitering and graffiti, if they choose. Bill 21 leaves these decisions in the hands of local government, where I believe they should be. It simply offers them one avenue to combat juvenile crime and delinquency if they feel it is needed in their community. In addition, this bill has been endorsed by the County Commissioners' Association. It is a noncontroversial bill that I hope you will support. Mr. Chairman, I renew my motion for the adoption of Senate Bill 21 on second reading."

"Are there questions or discussions?" Senator Jackson asked. "Hearing none, the question is on the passage of Senate Bill 21 on second reading. Those in favor, indicate by saying 'yea;' those opposed 'no.' The 'yeas' have it; Senate Bill 21 is passed on second reading."

The next bill on the calendar was Senate Bill 155, for a supplemental appropriation for public schools.

Senator Jackson: "The chair recognizes Senator Caucus."

Senator Caucus: "Mr. Chairman, there is a committee amendment to Senate Bill 155."

Senator Jackson: "The clerk will read the committee amendment."

The same procedure was followed as with Senate Bill 21. When the committee amendment was adopted, Senator Jackson again recognized Senator Caucus.

"Mr. Chairman, members of the Senate, I move the adoption of Senate Bill 155, as amended. I introduced this bill at the request of Governor Martinez, who asked for an additional $25 million in state funding for public schools. At the hearing in my committee, Senator Smith offered an amendment to increase state funding to $40 million. It was pointed out in our committee hearing that the State Budget Office now estimates that state revenues will be considerably higher than was anticipated at the time the governor made his request, and a $40 million appropriation for the state's public schools will not be a burden on the general fund," Senator Caucus said.

"Mr. Chairman, members of the Senate, I will be pleased to answer any questions about this legislation but, like the bill you just approved, this one is straightforward, uncomplicated. Many of the school districts of this state are experiencing significant increases in enrollment because of an unprecedented growth in population. We live in a state that has much appeal because of our quality of life. That translates to an influx of people from states that are not as fortunate as ours. And that, in turn, generates more retail sales and additional revenue from the state sales tax. Governor Martinez, recognizing all of these factors, has requested an increase in state funding for public schools. Your Appropriations committee agreed and increased the appropriation because of the latest estimates of the Budget Office. I could give you a number of additional reasons to support this bill, but I don't think they are necessary. Mr. Chairman, I renew my motion for the adoption of Senate Bill 155, as amended."

Senator Jackson called for a voice vote and Senate Bill 155 passed as amended.

When all the bills on second reading had been considered the Senate majority leader moved that "the committee rise and report." The motion was routinely adopted and Senator Trujillo resumed his position as chair. Senator Jackson, as chair of the Committee of the Whole, then moved that the Senate adopt the report of the Committee of the Whole. The motion was adopted, and the bills that passed on second reading were placed on the Senate's third reading calendar for final action.

The two bills that we are following—Senate Bills 21 and 155—were subsequently passed on third reading and sent to the House. In the House they went through the same process that we followed in the Senate: they were referred to committee, Senate Bill 21 to the House Local Government committee and Senate Bill 155 to the House Appropriations committee.

Senate Bill 21, concerned with juvenile delinquency in the counties, was reported to the House without amendment. It passed, with no changes from the Senate version, on second and third reading and was sent to the governor. Because the process in the House was the same that we followed in the Senate we will not follow that bill further. It was signed by the governor and became law.

Senate Bill 155, however, was amended by the House to provide $30 million in additional funds for public schools rather than the $40 million the Senate approved. Because of the different numbers in the House and Senate versions, we will have to take one more look at Senate Bill 155—in conference committee.

In the House

Only one of the bills we are tracking originated in the House—House Bill 15 by Representative Justice, concerning the sale of firearms. Her bill was reported, as amended, by the Judiciary committee and placed on the House calendar for second reading.

The House procedure for consideration of bills on second reading is the same as that in the Senate, and in all states—although there may be some variations from the procedures outlined here—it is customary for the House and Senate to follow the same procedures relating to the consideration of bills.

On the day that Representative Justice's firearms bill was on the second reading calendar, Representative Paul Konetsky, Speaker of the House, called the House to order and went through the agenda for that day until reaching the order of business entitled "Second Reading of House Bills."

At that point, Speaker Konetsky said, "The chair recognizes Representative Lee."

"Mr. Speaker," Representative Lee replied, "I move that the House resolve itself into the Committee of the Whole for the consideration of House bills on second reading."

"Without objection, so ordered," the Speaker responded.

When Representative Elizabeth Lee's motion that the House resolve itself into the Committee of the Whole was approved, she took the chair, called the committee to order, and requested the reading clerk to read House Bill 15, the first bill listed on that day's second reading calendar.

"House Bill 15, by Representative Justice," the clerk read, "a bill concerning the creation of the crime of unlawful sale of a firearm, reported as amended by the Judiciary committee."

"The chair recognizes Representative Lowery."

"Madam chair," Representative Lowery said, "there is a committee amendment to House Bill 15."

"The clerk will read the amendment."

"Committee amendment to House Bill 15," the reading clerk intoned. "On page 1, line 9, after the word 'years' delete the period, insert a semi-colon and add the phrase: 'provided, however, that a shotgun or rifle may be sold to a person under the age of eighteen years if such person has passed a state certified course on firearms safety.'"

"The chair recognizes Representative Lowery."

"I move the adoption of the committee amendment to House Bill 15. Madam Chair and members of the House, I hope that you will support this amendment. It was offered in committee by Representative Williams and was adopted on a vote of 9-2. House Bill 15, as introduced, banned the sale of any firearms—including shotguns and rifles—to anyone under the age of 18.

"I don't think I need to go into any detail concerning the constitutional arguments against this type of legislation; we have heard them more than once. This amendment represents a compromise between the two extreme positions in the ongoing controversy over banning the sale of firearms. This amendment would at least allow young people under 18 an opportunity to own firearms for hunting purposes. I renew my motion for the adoption of the committee amendment to House Bill 15," Representative Lowery concluded.

"The chair recognizes Representative Williams."

"Madam chair and members of the House, I don't need to elaborate on Representative Lowery's remarks. However, you should be aware that, even with my amendment, this bill barely made it out of the Judiciary committee. The vote was 6-5. So if you support this legislation, I think you would do well to vote for the committee amendment," Representative Williams said.

"The chair recognizes Representative Justice."

"Madam chair, members of the House," Representative Justice said, "I hope that you will support the committee amendment. I would have preferred that it not be added to the bill as introduced, but it does represent a workable compromise and I realize that without it, my bill probably would have very little chance of passage.

"Assuming the committee amendment is adopted, I would urge that you vote for the bill on second reading. If the bill is passed, as amended, we will not be going as far in banning the sale of firearms as I might have liked, but we will have taken a significant step in that direction."

On a division vote, the committee amendment was adopted and the bill was passed on second reading.

When the second reading calendar was completed, the majority floor leader moved that "the committee rise and report." The Speaker resumed the chair and the House voted to accept the report of the Committee of the Whole, which included the passage of House Bill 15, as amended. House Bill 15 was then placed on the calendar for third reading—final passage.

SUMMARY

Consideration of bills on the floor of the House and Senate is the most visible segment of the legislative process. It may also be the least understood by those not familiar with the operation of state legislatures. Legislative bodies conduct their business according to rules, statutes, or constitutional provisions designed to create an orderly process.

TABLE 7.1

Hearing of Bills—Senate

State	Committee Must Hear All Bills	Who Determines Which Bills Are Heard	Committees Must Report All Bills
Alabama	No	Committee chair	No
Alaska	No	Committee chair	No
Arizona	No	Committee chair	No
Arkansas	No	Committee chair	No
California	No response		
Colorado	Yes	Committee chair, author, member	Yes
Connecticut	No	Chair, author, member, petition	No
Delaware	No	Committee chair	No
Florida	No	Committee chair	No
Georgia	No	Committee chair, member	No
Hawaii	No	Committee chair	No
Idaho	No	Committee chair	Yes
Illinois	No	Committee chair, author	Yes
Indiana	No	Committee chair	No
Iowa	No	Committee chair, member	No
Kansas	No	Committee chair	No
Kentucky	No	Committee chair	No
Louisiana	No	Committee chair, author	No
Maine	Not required, usually do	Committee chair	Yes
Maryland	Yes		Yes
Massachusetts	Yes		Yes
Michigan	No	Committee chair	No
Minnesota	No	Committee chair, author	No
Mississippi	No	Committee chair, author, member	No
Missouri	No	Committee chair	No
Montana	Yes		No
Nebraska	Yes		No
Nevada	No	Committee chair	No
New Hampshire	Yes		Yes
New Jersey	No	Committee chair	No
New Mexico	No	Committee chair	No
New York	No	Committee chair	No
North Carolina	No response		
North Dakota	Not required, usually do	Committee chair	Yes
Ohio	No	Committee chair	No
Oklahoma	No	Committee chair	No
Oregon	No	Committee chair (1)	No
Pennsylvania	No	Committee chair	No
Rhode Island	No response		
South Carolina	No	Committee chair	No
South Dakota	Yes		Yes
Tennessee	Yes		No
Texas	No	Committee chair, author	No
Utah	Yes	Presiding officer	Yes
Vermont	No	Committee chair, author, member	No
Virginia	No	Committee chair	No
Washington	No	Committee chair	No
West Virginia	No	Committee chair, member	No
Wisconsin	No	Committee chair	No
Wyoming	No	Committee chair	No

Notes:

1. In Oregon, if two committee members provide the chair with at least 48 hours notice, a motion to place measures on the agenda for hearing must be considered by the committee at its next meeting. If the motion carries, a hearing will occur.

Source: Inside The Legislative Process, 1991 ed., American Society of Legislative Clerks and Secretaries and National Conference of State Legislatures.

TABLE 7.2

HEARING OF BILLS—HOUSE

State	Committee Must Hear All Bills	Who Determines Which Bills Are Heard	Committees Must Report All Bills
Alabama	No	Committee chair	No
Alaska	No	Committee chair	No
Arizona	No	Committee chair	No
Arkansas	Yes	NA	Yes
California	No	Committee chair	Yes
Colorado	Yes	NA	Yes
Connecticut	No	Chair, author, member, petition	No
Delaware	Yes	NA	No
Florida	No	Committee chair	No
Georgia	No	Committee chair, author	No
Hawaii	No	Committee chair, author, member	No
Idaho	No response		
Illinois	No	Committee chair, author	No
Indiana	No	Committee chair	Yes
Iowa	No	Committee chair	No
Kansas	No	Committee chair	No
Kentucky	No	Committee chair, author	No
Louisiana	No	Committee chair, author	No
Maine	No	Committee chair	Yes
Maryland	Yes, if time permits	Committee chair	No
Massachusetts	Yes	NA	Yes
Michigan	No		No
Minnesota	No	Committee chair	No
Mississippi	No	Committee chair	No
Missouri	No	Committee chair, author	No
Montana	Yes	NA	No
Nebraska	Not applicable--unicameral legislature		
Nevada	No	Committee chair	No
New Hampshire	Yes	NA	Yes
New Jersey	No	Committee chair, author, member	No
New Mexico	Yes	Presiding officer	No
New York	No	Author	No
North Carolina	Yes	Member	Yes
North Dakota	Not required, usually do	Committee chair	Yes
Ohio	No	Committee chair	No
Oklahoma	No	Committee chair, author	No
Oregon	No	Committee chair (1)	
Pennsylvania	No	Committee chair, author, member	No
Rhode Island	No response		
South Carolina	No	No response	No
South Dakota	Yes	NA	Yes
Tennessee	No	Committee chair, author	No
Texas	No	Committee chair	No
Utah	No	Committee chair	Yes
Vermont	No	Committee chair, member	No
Virginia	No	Committee chair	No
Washington	No	Committee chair	No
West Virginia	No	Committee chair	No
Wisconsin	No	Committee chair	No
Wyoming	No	Committee chair	No

Notes:

1. In the Oregon House, a majority of the members of a committee may request a public hearing or work session to be held on any measure in possession of the committee. The chair must schedule the hearing or session within 3 session days.

Source: Inside The Legislative Process, 1991 ed., American Society of Legislative Clerks and Secretaries and National Conference of State Legislatures.

TABLE 7.3

Mechanisms Used to Limit Debate

State	No Limits	Limit How Often A Member May Speak	Limit How Long A Member May Speak	Limit Both How Often and Long A Member May Speak	Description of Limit on How Often A Member May Speak	Description of Limit on Length of Members' Presentations
Alabama	S			B	S-Twice per motion; H-Once per	S-1 hour each time; H-10 minutes
Alaska	S	H-Spkr's option			H-Once if Speaker so states	
Arizona				H	H-Once; sponsor may open/close	H-5 minutes; sponsor-10 min each to open/close
Arkansas				B	B-Once per subject	S-1 hour; H-30 minutes
California				H	H-Once per measure	H-Open-5 min; each respondent- 2 min; close-5 min
Colorado	B			H-3rd reading	H-Twice	H-10 minutes
Connecticut	H					
Delaware		S			S-Up to 3 times per question	
Florida				S	S-Once on an issue	S-30 minutes; H-pro/con sides given equal time
Georgia			H	S	S-Twice	S-30 minutes; H-1 hour
Hawaii		S	H	H	B-Twice	H-10 minutes each time
Idaho	(1)					
Illinois		S		H	B-Once	H-5 min; sponsor 10 min to open/5 min to close
Indiana	H			S	B-Once	30 minutes
Iowa	S			H	H-Twice without leave	H-20 minute limit to close on a bill
Kansas		B			B-Twice	
Kentucky		H			S-Once; H-Twice on same subject	
Louisiana		S		S	S-Twice per subject; H-Once	S-30 minutes
Maine		B		H	S-Once; H-Twice without leave	H-15 minutes
Maryland	H	(2)			(2)	
Massachusetts	S			(3)		H-Certain circumstances-3 minutes or 500 words
Michigan		B		B	S-Twice per item; H-Once or twice	
Minnesota	S	H		H	H-Twice	
Mississippi				B	S-Twice per question; H-Once	S-20 min; H-10 min-main question, others-5 min
Missouri	S			H	H-Once	H-15 minutes
Montana	S			S	3 times per motion	5 minutes
Nebraska					B-Twice without leave	
Nevada		B			S-Once without leave; H-(4)	
New Hampshire		B			S-Twice; H-3 times	H-15 min on 1st & 2nd times; 5 min 3rd time
New Jersey				B	S-Once to explain vote; H-Once	S-5 minutes; H-3 hours
New Mexico				B	B-Twice on same subject	H-15 min each, plus 2 min to vote explanation
New York		S		H	S-Main question-twice; others-once;	S-Main question-30 min & 15 min; others-10 min
North Carolina				B		

TABLE 7.3 (CONTINUED)

MECHANISMS USED TO LIMIT DEBATE

State	No Limits	Limit How Often A Member May Speak	Limit How Long A Member May Speak	Limit Both How Often and Long A Member May Speak	Description of Limit on How Often A Member May Speak	Description of Limit on Length of Members' Presentations
North Dakota		S		B	Twice	10 minutes; then 5 minutes
Ohio				H	B-Twice per question	H-20 minutes per question, etc. per day
Oklahoma				B	H-Once per subject	H-10 minutes
Oregon		B		B	S-Once without leave; H-once	B-Carrier-10 minute open & close; others-5 min.
Pennsylvania	*					
Rhode Island		S	B		B-Twice	
South Carolina					S-Twice per question	B-10 minutes
South Dakota				H		
Tennessee	S			B	B-Twice	S-20 min; then 10 min; H-15 min; then 10 min
Texas		S		B	H-Twice on same question	H-20 min to open/close; 10 min for other speeches
Utah		B		H	B-Twice	S-President limit; usually to 2-5 minutes; H-(6)
Vermont		H			B-Twice without leave	
Virginia	S				H-Once until all others have spoken	
Washington				B	S-Once, generally; H-twice	B-3 minutes; usually used late in session
West Virginia		S		H	B-Twice without leave	H-Time limit determined by House
Wisconsin		B				
Wyoming				B	S-Twice per question; H-3 times	

Key:
B = Both Chambers
S = Senate or Council only
H = House or Assembly only
* = Did not respond to survey

Notes:
1. Idaho Senate limits debate in committee of the whole and on appeals.
2. Maryland senators may speak only once until every other senator wishing to speak has spoken. By 2/3 vote, the Senate also may limit debate.
3. Massachusetts House members generally are allowed 30 minutes on main questions; if no other member wishes to speak, the same member is allowed another 30 minutes. Debate is limited on certain questions; then members may speak once for 3 minutes.
4. New Hampshire House members cannot speak a second time unless all others who wish to speak have spoken a first time.
5. North Carolina House members may speak twice on a main motion (30 minutes, then 15 minutes) and twice on amendments (10 minutes, then 5 minutes).
6. In the Utah House, no member may speak longer than 15 minutes at any time, unless extended by majority vote. Floor time on any legislation may not exceed 8 hours.

CHAPTER

Conference Committees

It is in the conference committees where legislators resolve the differences between different versions of the same legislation passed by the House and Senate. In the following chapter, we will watch as Senator Caucus's Senate Bill 155 is discussed and the differences are resolved in conference committee.

Conference committees have been characterized as "little legislative bodies," which receive little public attention and little media coverage and yet wield tremendous power. Despite the relatively obscure nature of their work, conference committees play a major role in the legislative process. Bills that are enacted by both legislative chambers must be passed with exactly the same wording, or exactly the same numbers. There can be no differences, because there must not be any confusion about what the legislature intended when the legislation was enacted. The only state that never has this problem is Nebraska, which has a single chamber rather than the two found in all other states.

The mechanism used to resolve differences between a state's two legislative chambers is the conference committee. When a bill passes on third reading in the House, for example, it goes to the Senate for passage. In the Senate, the bill goes through the committee and floor processes that we discussed earlier. If the Senate makes changes to the House bill before passing it, the bill must be sent back to the House. The House then has two choices. It can accept the Senate version and re-enact the bill, or it can refuse to accept the Senate amendments and request a conference committee to resolve the differences.

Membership of a conference committee varies from six to as many as 10 or 12 legislators, depending on the state and legislation under consideration. The most common number of conferees is six, three from each legislative chamber. If the legislation in question involves appropriations, however, the membership of the conference committee may be more than the usual six. When there are six conferees, the normal procedure is to appoint four members from the majority party of each chamber and two from the minority, especially when a bill has had bipartisan support.

In most legislatures, conferees are appointed by the President of the Senate or the Speaker of the House. In a few chambers, they are appointed by the Lt. Governor, as the presiding officer (found in the Alabama, Idaho, Texas, Washington and West Virginia senates). In other states, conference committee members are appointed by the President *pro tem* of the Senate or the Speaker *pro tem* of the House. In a few state chambers, conferees are appointed by the majority leader, and in several states the minority leader appoints or has input into the appointment of minority party conferees. Whatever the method, the conferees most likely to be appointed include the chair of the standing committee that considered the bill, the bill's sponsor, and—in the case of a controversial bill—members who are strong supporters of the majority's position on the legislation.

A state legislative chamber determines the parameters of consideration for its conference committees. There are several methods for setting the scope of a conference committee: (1) The scope may be limited to the differences between the two chambers, (2) The entire bill may be subject to change, that is, the committee is free to make any changes it deems necessary, (3) The scope is limited unless the House or Senate, or both, vote to allow the conference committee to go beyond the differences, (4) The scope is limited for the first conference committee appointed, but if the first conference committee is unable to reach agreement, the scope is unlimited for any subsequent committees chosen to consider the same bill. A combination of these four options may also be found in effect, depending on the state legislative body.

The most common requirement for a conference committee to reach agreement is a majority vote of the conferees from each chamber. In some states a majority vote of all the conferees of both chambers, or of the House or Senate members, is required. In two states (Indiana and New Hampshire) a unanimous vote of all the members of a conference committee is necessary.

When agreement has been reached, the conference committee report goes to one of the chambers for action. The chamber which first considers the bill as agreed upon by the conference committee varies, depending on the state. In some states, the chamber where the bill originated acts first, in others the chamber that requested the conference committee acts first. In any event, both chambers must vote to accept the bill as agreed upon by the conference committee. When that occurs, the bill is sent to the governor.

If a conference committee cannot reach agreement, a new committee can be appointed; but when bills go to conference, there is always the possibility that final agreement cannot be reached—by the committee or by the vote in each chamber. In that case, the bill would die.

SENATE BILL 155 GOES TO CONFERENCE

The bill requested by Governor Martinez to increase state funding for public schools was amended as it went through the legislative process. As introduced by Senator Caucus, it called for an additional $25 million in state funding. At the Senate Appropriations committee hearing Senator Laurel Smith proposed an amendment to increase state funding to $40 million. Her amendment was adopted by the committee and, subsequently, by the Senate on second and third reading.

The House, however, amended the Senate bill to provide only $30 million.

When the House version was returned to the Senate, Senator Caucus moved to reject the House amendment and request a conference committee. His motion was adopted, and the President of the Senate appointed Senators Caucus, Smith and Jackson as the Senate conferees.

In the House, the Speaker appointed Representatives Warnock, Williams and Wattenberg to the committee.

The conference committee met the following day. In this case, the committee was able to reach agreement quickly.

"Look, we're not that far apart," Senator Caucus suggested, "and each chamber has approved more funding than the governor requested. Why don't we just split the difference and go with $35 million? There will certainly be enough money available to fund that amount, and I think there is general agreement that state funding for schools should be increased—it's just a matter of the amount."

After a brief discussion, the committee agreed unanimously on $35 million. "That was easy," Representative Wattenberg commented. "I hope the next conference committee I'm on goes that smoothly."

The conference committee report on Senate Bill 155 was sent to the House, where it was adopted on a roll-call vote. It then went to the Senate where Senator Caucus moved its adoption. His motion also passed on a roll-call vote. The bill was enrolled and sent to the governor.

SUMMARY

Both chambers of a legislature must pass exactly the same version of a bill. When a bill that originated in the Senate, for example, is amended by the House, the Senate can accept or reject the House amendments. If the House amendments are rejected, the differences between the two versions must be settled by a conference committee appointed for that purpose. When conference committee reports are adopted by both chambers, the bill is enacted. If agreement on the same version cannot be reached, the bill is dead.

TABLE 8.1

CRITERIA USED TO APPOINT CONFERENCE COMMITTEES

State	Criteria are used to appoint conference committees	Bill sponsor, author, or carrier	Chair of the standing committee with jurisdiction	Member of the standing committee with jurisdiction	Proportional party representation	At least one minority party representative	Majority of appointees originally voted in favor of the bill	At least one appointee originally voted against the bill	Other
Alabama	No								
Alaska	Both	Both	Both	Both	Both	Both			
Arizona	Both	Both	Both	House	House	Senate			
Arkansas	House	House						House	
California	Both	Senate	Senate	Senate	Senate	Senate	House	Both	
Colorado	Both	Both				Both			Both
Connecticut	Both		Senate	Senate		Both		Both	
Delaware	NA								
Florida	Both	Senate	Both	Both	Both		House		
Georgia	Yes								
Hawaii	Both		Both		House				House
Idaho	Senate	Senate	Senate	Senate	Senate	Senate			
Illinois	Both	Both	Both	Senate	Senate	Both			House
Indiana	Both	Both				House			House
Iowa	House	House	Both	Both	House	Both			
Kansas	Both	Senate			Senate	Both			
Kentucky	No								
Louisiana	House	House	House						House
Maine	Both	Both	House						Both
Maryland	Both	Both	House	Both			Senate		
Massachusetts	*								
Michigan	Both	Senate	Both	Both		Both			
Minnesota	Senate	Senate		Senate		Senate			
Mississippi	*								
Missouri	Both	Both			House				
Montana	No								
Nebraska	NA								
Nevada	Both						Both		
New Hampshire	Both	Both	Senate	Both		Senate			House
New Jersey	No								
New Mexico	Both		House	House	Both	Both			
New York	Senate	Senate	House	House		Senate			House

TABLE 8.1 (CONTINUED)

CRITERIA USED TO APPOINT CONFERENCE COMMITTEES

State	Criteria are used to appoint conference committees	Bill sponsor, author, or carrier	Chair of the standing committee with jurisdiction	Member of the standing committee with jurisdiction	Proportional party representation	At least one minority party representative	Majority of appointees originally voted in favor of the bill	At least one appointee originally voted against the bill	Other
North Carolina	House	House	House				House		Both
North Dakota	Both	Both	House			Both			Both
Ohio	Both	House		Senate		Both			
Oklahoma	Both	Senate	Senate	Senate	Senate				
Oregon	Both	Senate	Senate		Both	Senate			House
Pennsylvania	Both	Both				House			
Rhode Island	*								
South Carolina	House	Both	House	House	House			Both	
South Dakota	Both	Senate						Senate	
Tennessee	Senate	Both						House	Senate
Texas	Both	Senate		Senate	Senate	Both	House		House
Utah	Both	House				House	House		
Vermont	House	Both	House	House	House	House	House	House	
Virginia	Both	Both	House	House	House	Both	House	Both	
Washington	Both	Both	Both	Both	Both	House	Both	Both	
West Virginia	Both	House	Senate	House		Both			
Wisconsin	Both	Both				Both	Both		
Wyoming	Both						Both	Both	

* Did not respond to survey.

Source: National Conference of State Legislatures, preliminary information from ASLCS comprehensive survey, February 1996.

TABLE 8.2

NUMBER OF MEMBERS APPOINTED TO CONFERENCE COMMITTEES

State	Non-Fiscal Conference Committee		Fiscal Conference Committee	
	Senate	House	Senate	House
Alabama	3	3	3	3
Alaska	3	3	3	3
Arizona	3-5	3-5	3-5	3-5
Arkansas	Varies	Varies	Varies	Varies
California	3	3	3	3
Colorado	3	3	3	3
Connecticut	3	3	3	3
Delaware	NA	NA	NA	NA
Florida	3-5	3-5	10-14	10-14
Georgia	3	3	3	3
Hawaii	3-5	3-7	Ways & Means members	Finance members
Idaho	Usually 3	Usually 3	Usually 3	Usually 3
Illinois	5	5	5	5
Indiana	2	2	2	2
Iowa	5	5	5	5
Kansas	3	3	3	3
Kentucky	3	3	3 or more	3 or more
Louisiana	3	3	3	3
Maine	3	3	3	3
Maryland	3	3	3	3
Massachusetts	*			
Michigan	3	3	3	3
Minnesota	3 or 5	3 or 5	3 or 5	3 or 5
Mississippi	3	3	3	3
Missouri	5	5	5	5
Montana	3	3	3	3
Nebraska	NA	NA	NA	NA
Nevada	3	3	3	3
New Hampshire	3	4	3	4 or 5
New Jersey	3	3	3	3
New Mexico	3	3	3	3
New York	5 or more	5 or more	5 or more	5 or more
North Carolina		3-5		21
North Dakota	3	3	3	3
Ohio	3	3	3	3
Oklahoma	3	3	Varies	Varies
Oregon	3	2-3	3	3
Pennsylvania	3	3	3	3
Rhode Island	*			
South Carolina	3	3	3	3
South Dakota	3	3	3	3
Tennessee	3-5		Ways & Means members	
Texas	5	5	5	5
Utah	3	3	3	3
Vermont	3	3	3	3
Virginia	3	3	4	4
Washington	3	3	3	3
West Virginia	3	3	5	5
Wisconsin	3	3	3	3
Wyoming	3	3	5	5

* Did not respond to survey.
Source: National Conference of State Legislatures, preliminary information from the ASLCS comprehensive survey, February 1996.

TABLE 8.3

Vote for Report to Be Adopted by Conference Committee and Signatures Required

State	Majority of the conferees from each chamber	Majority vote of all conferees	Unanimous vote of conferees	Other	Conference committee chairs must sign	Equal number of conferees from each chamber must sign	Majority of conferees from each body must sign	Majority of all conferees must sign	All conferees must sign	Other
Alabama	Both						Both			
Alaska	Both							Both		
Arizona	House									House
Arkansas	Both	House			House		Both			House
California	Senate						Both			
Colorado	Both								Both	
Connecticut	NA									
Delaware	Both						Both			
Florida	Both						House			
Georgia	House						Both			
Hawaii	Both						Both		House	
Idaho	Both				Senate			Both		
Illinois		Both					Both			
Indiana	Both		Both							
Iowa	Both			Senate				Both		Both
Kansas	House						Both		House	
Kentucky	Both	Both						Both		
Louisiana		Both					Both			
Maine	Both	Both		House			Both			
Maryland	*									
Massachusetts							Both			
Michigan	Both						Both			
Minnesota	Both						House			
Mississippi	House									House
Missouri	Both	Both					Both			
Montana	Both						Both			
Nebraska	NA								Senate	
Nevada	Both						House			

111

TABLE 8.3 (CONTINUED)

Vote for Report to Be Adopted by Conference Committee and Signatures Required

State	Majority of the conferees from each chamber	Majority vote of all conferees	Unanimous vote of conferees	Other	Conference committee chairs must sign	Equal number of conferees from each chamber must sign	Majority of conferees from each body must sign	Majority of all conferees must sign	All conferees must sign	Other
New Hampshire			Both							
New Jersey		House						House		
New Mexico	Both						Senate			
New York	House				House					
North Carolina	House				House		House			
North Dakota	Both						Both			
Ohio	Both						Both			
Oklahoma	House						Both		House	
Oregon	Both						Both			
Pennsylvania	Both						Both			
Rhode Island	*			House						
South Carolina	Both						Both			House
South Dakota	Senate						Senate			
Tennessee	Both				Senate		Both			
Texas	Both						House			
Utah	Both						Both			
Vermont	Both						Both			
Virginia		Both						Senate	House	
Washington	Both						Both		House	
West Virginia	Both							Both		
Wisconsin	Both					House				
Wyoming	Both						Both			Senate

* Did not respond to survey.

Source: National Conference of State Legislatures, preliminary information from ASLCS comprehensive survey, February 1996.

TABLE 8.4

CONSIDERATION AND VOTE ON CONFERENCE REPORT; JOINT RULES

State	Chamber That First Considers Report	Vote Required to Adopt Report	Roll Call Required	Joint Rules
Alabama	Originating	S-Original bill vote;		
		H-Majority elected	B	Yes
Alaska	Varies	Original bill vote	B	Yes
Arizona	Non-originating	Majority present		No
Arkansas	Originating	Majority elected		No
California	Varies	S-Depends if report changes vote requirement		
		H-Original bill vote	B	Yes
Colorado	Non-originating	Majority elected	B	Yes
Connecticut	At the same time in both	Majority present	B	Yes
Delaware	NA			
Florida	Varies	Majority present	S	No
Georgia		Majority elected		No
Hawaii	Varies	Majority elected	S	No
Idaho	Originating	Majority present		?
Illinois	Varies	Original bill vote	B	No
Indiana	Varies	Majority elected	B	Yes
Iowa	Originating	Majority present		No
Kansas	Non-originating	S-Original bill vote;		
		H-Majority elected	B	Yes
Kentucky	Varies	Majority present	S	No
Louisiana	Usually originating	Original bill vote	B	No
Maine	Requesting	Majority present		Yes
Maryland	Requesting	Majority present	B	?
Massachusetts	*			
Michigan	Originating	Original bill vote	B	Yes
Minnesota	Originating	S-Majority elected		
		H-Majority present	B	Yes
Mississippi	Varies	Original bill vote	H	Yes
Missouri	Originating	Majority elected	B	?
Montana	Varies	Majority present	B	Yes
Nebraska	NA	NA	NA	NA
Nevada	Originating	S-Voice vote;		
		H-Majority present	B	Yes
New Hampshire	Non-originating	Majority present		Yes
New Jersey		Majority elected	H	Yes
New Mexico	Varies	Majority present		Yes
New York				Yes
North Carolina	Varies	Original bill vote	H	No
North Dakota	Originating	Majority present	B	Yes
Ohio	Varies	Original bill vote	B	No
Oklahoma	Originating	S-Majority present		
		H-Majority elected	H	Yes
Oregon	Originating	S-Majority elected		
		H-Majority present	B	No
Pennsylvania	Originating	Original bill vote	B	No
Rhode Island	*			
South Carolina	Originating	Majority present		No
South Dakota	Originating	Original bill vote	B	No
Tennessee	Originating	Majority elected	B	No
Texas	Varies	S-Usually majority present		
		H-Original bill vote		No
Utah	Non-originating	Original bill vote	H	Yes
Vermont	Non-originating	Majority present		Yes
Virginia	Chamber possessing papers	S-Majority voting but not less than 16		
		H-Original bill vote	B	No

TABLE 8.4 (CONTINUED)

CONSIDERATION AND VOTE ON CONFERENCE REPORT; JOINT RULES

State	Chamber That First Considers Report	Vote Required to Adopt Report	Roll Call Required	Joint Rules
Washington	Non-originating	Majority present	B	?
West Virginia	Originating	Majority present	H	Yes
Wisconsin	Non-originating	Majority present	B	?
Wyoming	Originating	Majority elected	S	Yes

Key:
Originating = the chamber in which the bill was originally introduced (i.e., House for House bill)
Non-originating = the opposite chamber from which the bill was originally introduced (i.e., Senate for House bill)
Requesting = the chamber refusing to concur in amendments and requesting the conference committee
Majority elected = by a majority of the members elected to the chamber
Majority present = by a majority of those members present and voting
Original bill vote = by the vote required to pass the original bill (i.e., majority vote for a bill that required a majority vote originally; two-thirds vote for a bill that required two-thirds vote originally)

* Did not respond to survey
Source: National Conference of State Legislatures, preliminary information from the ASLCS comprehensive survey, February 1996.

CHAPTER

Governor's Choice

When bills have been passed by both chambers of the legislature, the next action is up to the governor—who has several choices that will be outlined in this chapter. These choices of action will be exemplified by Governor Martinez as he considers three bills we've been following, Senate Bill 21, Senate Bill 155, and House Bill 15.

This book is about the state *legislative* process. So where does the governor get into the act? Bills are passed by the legislature, but in 49 of the 50 states they don't become law until the governor has his say. North Carolina is the only state whose governor does not have the veto power, so in that state bills become law on final passage by the legislature. Following the 1996 election, however, the governor of North Carolina may have the veto power. At the 1995 session of the North Carolina legislature a proposal to amend the state constitution to give the governor the power to veto bills passed and will be on that state's ballot in November 1996. If the amendment passes, North Carolina will join the other 49 states in giving the governor the power to veto bills passed by the legislature.

After bills have passed both houses of the legislature, they are **enrolled** and sent to the governor. In every state where the governor has the veto power, there is a time limit for the governor to take action. Generally, the governor has from five to ten days to make a decision. The clock begins to tick in some states when the bill is delivered to the governor, in others on final passage. A few states provide for a pocket veto; that is, if the legislature completes its business and ends the session before the governor has time to act on the legislation, the governor may simply "pocket" the bill—take no action—and the bill dies.

Depending on the state, the governor has several courses of action after a bill has passed both chambers of the legislature:

- The governor can sign the bill. If so, it becomes law. It may not become effective, however, until a later date. In some states, unless there is a date included in the bill, it becomes effective when it is signed by the governor. In others, unless the bill sets a different date, it takes effect at a later time, usually after the legislature has adjourned and frequently at the beginning of a state's fiscal year. In Minnesota, for example, the **effective date** is August 1, except for appropriations bills. The effective date for those is July 1, coinciding with the beginning of the state's fiscal year.
- The governor can express disagreement with the legislation by not signing it, in which case it becomes law without the governor's signature after a specified time.
- The governor can veto the bill. When that occurs, the legislature has an opportunity to override the veto. Typically the governor sends a veto message, with the reasons for that action, to the legislative chamber in which the bill originated. The legislature then has the option of accepting the governor's veto or attempting to override it. In most states, a two-thirds vote is required to override a veto. So if a state had 120 members in the House and 60 in the Senate, a vote of 80 in the House and 40 in the Senate would be necessary to override a veto and enact the legislation over the governor's objections.

If the legislative leaders believe they do not have the necessary votes to override, however, they might decide not to bring the question up, and the governor's veto would stand without further action by the legislature.

THE GOVERNOR'S CHOICE ON THREE BILLS

Three of the bills we have been tracking passed both houses and were sent to Governor Martinez. The governor agreed with two of the bills: Senate Bill 21, Senator Brian Caucus's bill giving counties the power to adopt ordinances relating to loitering and graffiti by juveniles, and imposing

CHAPTER 10

Congress

Even though the emphasis of this book is on the legislative process in the 50 states, in this chapter we will look at the legislative process at the federal level—the U.S. Congress—where laws are made that affect the citizens of all 50 states. We will also illustrate comparisons and contrasts between the federal and state legislative processes.

The lawmaking process is basically the same, whether at the state or federal level. In Congress, bills are introduced, and assigned to committees. Committees, in turn schedule public hearings, amend or perhaps rewrite the bill, and either kill it in committee or report it for consideration by the full membership of the legislative chamber. If it passes in one house, it goes to the other chamber, where the process is repeated. If the two chambers pass different versions of the same bill the differences must be resolved, usually by a conference committee, and both chambers must then pass the final version of the bill by adopting the conference committee report. When a bill has been passed, it goes to the president for approval or a veto. If a bill is vetoed, Congress has an opportunity to override the veto.

Even though the basic procedures are similar, there are a number of differences between Congress and the states. A major difference involves the place Congress occupies in our system of government. As we explained in an earlier chapter, Congress is responsible for enacting laws that apply to all 50 states, while state legislatures pass laws that affect only one state.

Congress has authority under the Constitution to pass laws affecting the general welfare of the people and to make all laws necessary to carry out the responsibilities given to Congress in Article I of the Constitution. Those powers that are not specified in the Constitution as belonging to Congress are reserved to the states. The power of Congress has expanded over the years, however, especially during periods of national crisis. After the Civil War, Congress passed laws to ensure that the civil rights of individuals would be protected in all of the states. During one of the nation's major economic crises, the Great Depression of the 1930s, Congress expanded its scope to include a broad array of national economic policy, such as the Social Security System. And Congress continues to respond to national interest groups and passes laws affecting everything from arts and education to crime and welfare.

There is considerable difference, as you might expect, in the size of Congress as compared to state legislatures. There are 535 members of Congress: 435 in the House; 100 in the Senate. Each state regardless of population has two senators. The number of members in the House from each state is determined by population. The most populous state, California, has 52 House members; several less populous states, Wyoming and Montana for example, have only one representative in the House but two in the Senate.

This arrangement, equal representation for each state in the Senate and representation in the House according to a state's population, was the result of a compromise arrived at by delegates to the Constitutional Convention in 1787. Delegates from the small states feared that if the number of members from each state in both houses of Congress were determined according to a state's population, the populous states would dominate the national legislature. Because of the compromise finally agreed upon at Philadelphia in 1787, California, with 31 million residents has two votes in the Senate as does Wyoming, with a population of 465,000.

Senators are elected state-wide. In states with more than one House seat, House members are elected from districts as nearly equal as possible in population. In state legislatures, both Senate and House members are elected from districts based on population. Most state legislatures have far fewer members than the U.S. Congress. The only state chamber that comes close to Congress is the New Hampshire House, which has 400 members.

BY THE NUMBERS

Every 10 years, the United States Census Bureau mounts an enormous effort to count every one of the more than 260 million Americans. Even though the information gathered by the census is used for many different things, the only reason the U.S. Constitution mandates a census is so Congress can determine the number of seats each state will get in the U.S. House of Representatives. This process is called reapportionment.

Reapportionment begins when the Clerk of the U.S. House of Representatives takes the official census data and feeds it into a formula. The formula guarantees that each state will get at least one seat in the U.S. House and that the remaining seats will be allocated to the states based on their population. Following the release of the 1990 census data, California was awarded 52 seats in Congress, up from 45 seats after the 1980 census. The 1990 reapportionment left seven states with only one seat in the U.S. House: Alaska, Delaware, Vermont, North Dakota, South Dakota, Wyoming, and Montana. The only state in this group to lose a seat was Montana, which had two U.S. House seats after the 1980 census.

Following the reapportionment that determines the number of seats each state gets in Congress, the state legislatures—and in a few cases,

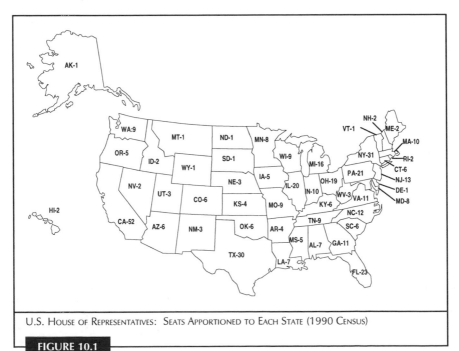

U.S. HOUSE OF REPRESENTATIVES: SEATS APPORTIONED TO EACH STATE (1990 CENSUS)

FIGURE 10.1

special commissions—set about the task of redistricting. Redistricting is the process of resetting the boundaries of the districts that elect legislators to lawmaking bodies. All districts for representative lawmaking bodies, whether it is the U.S. House of Representatives, the state legislature, or the town council, must be redrawn at least once every 10 years following the release of new census data. This is because the United States Supreme Court found in a series of rulings in the mid-60s that the Constitution requires relative numerical equality between districts. In other words, each representative in the U.S. House must represent roughly the same number of people so that each citizen's voice is equally represented in debates on potential laws. This concept is known as "one person, one vote" and it applies to all legislative bodies in the U.S. except for the U.S. Senate, which is specifically established in the Constitution as the body where states are represented equally—not according to population.

The process of redrawing district boundaries has become extremely political. Politicians have learned that they can draw districts filled with mostly Democrats or mostly Republicans, thus increasing the chances that one party or the other will win the seat. This practice occasionally results in some bizarre-shaped districts. Oddly shaped districts have become known as **gerrymanders** since 1812, when a cartoonist for the *Boston Gazette* bestowed the term on a strangely shaped district drawn by then Massachusetts' Governor Elbridge Gerry to achieve a partisan advantage. Ever since, state legislators have been drawing unusually shaped districts to further their political goals.

In recent years, many states have had new district lines challenged in court as violating the rights of protected minority groups such as African Americans. States must now comply with the 1965 Voting Rights Act by drawing districts with a majority of a minority group anywhere that there is a large enough concentration of a specific minority living in the same area. These districts, known as **majority, minority districts,** will typically elect a member of the minority group as its representative. When state legislatures are drawing district lines, the computers they use tell them the number of whites, African-Americans, Hispanics, etc. that will be in a new district. Under the Voting Rights Act, legislatures have created districts where over 50% of the voting age population in a new district will be minority. Legislatures cannot over-populate districts with minority residents or the maps would "waste" or "pack" minority voters and be in violation of the Voting Rights Act. Because many of these districts have been created in the past few years, the numbers of minority representatives in Congress and state legislatures have swelled to record levels.

COMMITTEES AND CONGRESSIONAL STAFF

Another difference between Congress and the state legislatures is in the committee structure. Much of the work of both state legislatures and Congress takes place in committee. But while state legislatures operate with relatively few standing committees and fewer subcommittees, Congress has an excessive number of committees: 39 standing committees in the Senate and House, and 154 subcommittees. Committee hearings and deliberations consume much more time in Congress than in the states. The whole Congressional legislative process, in fact, is much lengthier and more complicated than in the states. The national defense budget is an example: more than 100 separate House and Senate hearings may be necessary before it goes to the floor for action.

The increase in the number of committees has contributed to a huge increase in staff. Estimates of the total number of Congressional staff go as high as 23,000. Legislative staffs in the states range from 19 in Wyoming, to about 4,000 in New York.

Standing Committees

U.S. Congress—Senate

Agriculture
Appropriations
Armed Services
Banking, Housing and Urban Affairs
Budget
Commerce, Science and Transportation
Energy and Natural Resources
Environment and Public Works
Finance, Foreign Relations
Government Affairs
Indian Affairs
Judiciary
Labor and Human Resources
Nutrition and Forestry
Rules
Small Business
Veterans' Affairs
Select Committee on Ethics
Select Committee on Intelligence
Special Committee on Aging

Much of the work that is accomplished by the members of Congress is actually done by staff members working amongst themselves under the direction of their representative or senator. For example, when it is reported that the president negotiated with members of Congress on legislation, it does not necessarily mean that the president met personally with the members. On some special occasions, the president does meet with various members. The more common practice, however, is that a legislative liaison from the White House political office met with the

Standing Committees

U.S. Congress—House

Agriculture
Appropriations
Banking and Financial Services
Budget
Commerce
Economic and Educational
    Opportunities
Government Reform and Oversight
House Oversight
Intelligence
International Relations
Judiciary
National Security
Resources
Rules
Science
Small Business
Standards of Official Conduct
Transportation and Infrastructure
Veterans' Affairs
Ways and Means

member of Congress or with the staff person responsible for dealing with the issue under consideration. And frequently, much of the ground work for the negotiations that occur during the conference committee phase of the legislative process is laid by staff of the Senate and House committees involved, or by a member's personal staff.

Committee hearings held by a House or Senate committee often attract members who are especially interested in the legislation being considered. When members have a schedule conflict, a staff person may be assigned to observe the hearing and give the member a report. Usually the staff of the member will also assist in briefing the member on the issue and help frame questions that the member may want to ask of the witnesses at a hearing. Sometimes a House or Senate hearing may proceed even though only one member is present to hear the testimony. In these instances the "court reporter," who transcribes the testimony, is called upon to give the absent members a transcript of the hearing. Eventually this material is also made available to the public.

In addition to their offices in Washington, D.C., members of Congress maintain district offices in their home states. The major responsibility of staff persons in these offices is to respond to inquiries from constituents concerning government programs or to provide help to home-state residents who may be having problems with the federal bureaucracy.

ON THE FLOOR

Consideration of bills on the floor follows essentially the same procedure in both state legislatures and Congress, including first, second, and third readings. One major difference is in the U.S. House. Bills that come to the floor of the House do so under a rule adopted by the House Rules committee. A high percentage of the bills that reach the floor come under a "closed" rule which prohibits amendments other than those of the committee that considered the bill. The Rules committee also sets a time limit for debate. Floor debate, especially in the House, usually doesn't result in many members changing their votes. Lengthy committee consideration of legislation often results in the resolution of problems before a bill goes to the floor. Committee chairs and bill sponsors usually have a good vote count before they bring legislation to the floor. Although floor debate seldom changes many votes, it does serve a crucial purpose: floor debate provides members an opportunity to make a record regarding **legislative intent**, a factor the courts consider when interpreting the law.

When legislation that has been enacted by Congress is challenged in the courts, one of the factors the courts consider is the intent of Congress when it enacted the legislation. In determining the intent of Congress, the courts consider the legislative history of a bill, which includes transcripts of committee hearings, the committee report concerning the bill in question, and floor debate when the bill was considered in the House and Senate. In Congress, the debate is recorded in the *Congressional Record*. To clarify the intent of Congress, members provide detailed explanations of the bill, including answers to questions that may be posed solely for the purpose of establishing congressional intent.

With fewer members, the U. S. Senate makes more allowance for amendments by individual members, and more discussion during floor consideration. One result is that more legislation is written on the floor than is possible in the House. In that context, most state legislative bodies—both House and Senate—operate more like the U.S. Senate than the U.S. House.

CONFLICT AND COMPROMISE

The Congress is an institution built around the idea of conflict and compromise. While representatives from the state of Texas are interested in promoting increased prices for energy products to ensure continued production, representatives from the northeastern states, which are net energy consumers, hope to encourage lower prices for energy so that their constituents can afford heating bills.

Congress is not strictly a majoritarian institution. That is, during the course of debate and deliberation on a bill, the majority does not continually prevail. Among the forces that protect minority interest groups from being constantly overridden are the **filibuster** and the veto. Under rules of the Senate, members may filibuster a bill to prevent its passage. The filibuster can be initiated by one member. As long as that member can persuade 41 other members to support the filibuster, the legislation can be kept off the floor for a vote. The threat of a filibuster, therefore, often forces proponents of legislation to enlist at least 60 members to ensure its passage in the Senate, rather than the mere 51 votes needed for a majority. Also, the veto is a power given to the president under the Constitution. In order for the Congress to override a presidential veto, the proponents of the legislation must have two-thirds of the votes of the House of Representatives and the Senate.

Another check on congressional action is the two-step process for approving funding for various projects. First, a committee of Congress must approve legislation authorizing a program. The "authorization" process spells out the details of the program. For example, when the Office of Juvenile Justice and Delinquency was reauthorized by the Congress, the committees having jurisdiction of the agency worked to redefine its mission. They proposed a new method to fund a variety of programs relating to the overrepresentation of minorities among the institutionalized population and the need to give greater attention to young-women offenders. The next step to ensure the success of the authorized program is for one of the appropriations committees to actually appropriate the funds for the program. Although the appropriations committees are not generally concerned with programmatic changes, they often influence the nature of a program by deciding whether or not to fund the program. In the above case, an appropriations committee never authorized the spending for the new program. Therefore, it simply languished on the books.

Finally, the Constitution installs another element to place a check on Congress: the power of the federal courts to declare an act unconstitutional. If a law is declared unconstitutional, Congress may not be able to correct the defect. The only way to bring about the change sought by the proponents of the law, therefore, is through a **constitutional amendment**. For example, the proponents of a law to make desecration of the American flag a crime were denied statutory remedy when the Supreme Court said the law was unconstitutional. Given that setback, they sought to have their views become law by changing the Constitution.

The lesson to be learned from a recitation of roadblocks to federal legislation is that the framers of the Constitution were concerned that a Congress might be too active. The nation's founders had originally been concerned that the Articles of Confederation, a precursor to the Constitution, had not given sufficient power to the central government. And when they established a strong central government with defined powers over currency, commerce, and foreign affairs, they took great pains to tie the hands of Congress.

A closer look at the Violent Crime Control and Law Enforcement Act, an actual law enacted in 1994, will give you a better idea of how these forces can interact and produce an ambitious piece of legislation. It will also give you a detailed look at the legislative process at the congressional level.

A CASE STUDY OF MAJOR CONGRESSIONAL LEGISLATION

President Clinton signed the Violent Crime Control and Law Enforcement Act (VCCLEA) in a ceremony at the White House on September 13, 1994. Behind him was a bank of law enforcement officers in uniform and other dignitaries, including members of Congress. Scores of American flags fluttered in the background. The president proclaimed the legislation to be a victory for bi-partisanship. Yet the road to achieving the legislation was not as smooth as the pen strokes that were used to sign the bill.

While running for office in 1992, Clinton had stated his intention of proposing legislation that would ensure that 100,000 additional law enforcement officers would be placed on the streets of towns and cities across the land. The House and Senate each responded differently to public demands for increased safety from crime. In early 1993, crime bills were introduced in the House and were referred to the Judiciary committee. In the Senate, a bill that resembled one that had failed to pass in the previous Congress was introduced. As committees are under no explicit time frame to complete their review of legislation, attention was directed to more pressing legislative goals, including a major deficit-reduction package that was approved in the summer of 1993. Given the climate of deficit reduction, the most expensive crime package was optimistically calling for doubling federal expenditures to cut crime—up to $1 billion.

On November 2, 1993, both the Republican and Democratic parties thought they heard a warning thunderclap from the voters in the ousting of Democratic governors in Virginia and New Jersey. Although many factors, including economics and taxation, contributed to the election of Republican governors in each of these states, many news analysts and political party officials saw the election of Republicans as confirmation that legislation to prevent or reduce crime was a priority with voters. Overnight, the House and Senate began moving crime legislation.

The House used its Judiciary committee to consider several crime bills limited to specific issues and passed four bills on November 3. These bills included $3.5 billion for the president's COPS initiative as well as another $300 million for state prison drug treatment programs and for the suppression of the activities of gangs. After the November election the House considered several more bills, including a ban on the possession of handguns by youths and measures to end violence against women.

The Senate, in contrast, bypassed the committee process and brought an omnibus crime bill directly to the floor of the Senate. An omnibus bill is all-encompassing. It may contain several separately introduced bills on the same subject, folded into a single (omnibus) bill. During the debate on the crime bill, senators convinced themselves that they were not spending enough tax dollars on crime. As luck would have it, only weeks earlier they had approved a bill to reduce the size of the federal government by 250,000 workers. Senators saw this savings as a perfect opportunity to spend more money elsewhere and thus began a series of amendments to the crime bill that eventually resulted in legislation calling for spending $22 billion on federal crime-reduction programs. Amendments were made from the floor over the course of several days of debate. With the gate of the federal treasury open on a scale that had rarely occurred before, nearly any member of the Senate could propose an amendment successfully. Amendments to increase spending on crime reduction came from across the political spectrum; they were not the work of either political party.

By the end of November 1993 the House and Senate had each condemned crime through legislation that would cost billions of dollars. The public, they said, wanted swift and serious legislation to deal with the problem of crime. After 10 more months of bargaining, each chamber finally passed the same version of the bill and sent it to the president.

What happened in those 10 months helps to further clarify the competing pressures found in Congress—pressures that bring together legislators from highly contrasting areas of the nation. Most importantly, the president had to contend with members of his own party who disagreed with his endorsement of a national ban on ownership of assault weapons. Action on that element of the crime bill was postponed by the House because of controversy over the banning of guns, even though the Senate had already approved a ban on assault weapons. The House Judiciary committee completed work on a series of crime bills in March and bundled them together for a vote on the floor.

The Senate bill began as Senate 1607, but upon final approval, it was offered as a substitute for one of the House bills that had passed, H.R. 3355, which provided for building prisons and funding additional police officers at the local level in an effort to prevent crime. Procedurally, the

Senate had made it possible for the House to reconsider H.R. 3355, as amended. If the House approved the amended version, the bill could be sent directly to the president. The House Judiciary committee, however, was determined to craft its own version of an all-inclusive crime bill, and did so by April 21, 1994.

Once the House Judiciary committee approved the bill, it needed to be considered by the Rules committee. The Rules committee, one of the most powerful House committees, sets the rules for debating legislation on the House floor. The Rules committee also decides what amendments will be allowed during floor debate. Legislators plead with the Rules committee to be permitted to offer their amendments during the floor debate. Among the proposals sought to be included in the debate on the crime bill was one creating national rules to regulate the licensing of security guards, a traditional responsibility of state government. The amendment was allowed but was defeated when offered on the floor.

Once the Rules committee finishes its work, the full House of Representatives is allowed the opportunity to debate the bill and amendments, according to the rules established by the committee. When the complete package of crime legislation was considered by the House, it was approved by a vote of 284-141. Yet the most difficult part of the legislative process, arriving at a compromise between the House and Senate versions, had not even begun. So while the Senate passed its bill in November 1993 and the House passed its version five months later, on April 21, 1994, the bill still had months to go before it would reach the president's desk.

Members of the House and Senate were selected by their leadership to resolve the differences between the two versions. As in the state legislatures, the panel that meets to resolve the differences between a bill that has passed both chambers of a legislative body is called a conference committee. The conference committee includes members of the committees that considered the legislation earlier, when it was being debated and voted upon in each chamber. The members from each chamber have a vested interest in seeing that the bill comes out of the conference committee looking most like the version that was previously approved by their chamber. Normally, the conference committee comes too late in the legislative process to propose new items or additional spending to the legislation. Yet when the two versions of the crime legislation were compared, each had allowed more money for different items. The Senate version weighed in at about $22.3 billion, and the House version came in at a cost of close to $28 billion. When the dust cleared, the crime bill's cost was even higher—$30.2 billion.

When the bill went from the conference committee back to the House, some members were concerned about the assault weapon ban while others claimed that too much money had been added to the bill in conference. The issue of a federally funded midnight basketball program to keep juveniles off the streets became a political buzzword for what some considered to be unnecessary spending. A number of members from the president's own party opposed the bill because of its ban on assault weapons. The initial vote in the House to reconsider the bill failed. The president began negotiating with a group of moderate Republicans to allay some of their concerns about the spending for prevention programs, and after he agreed to group a variety of programs into a multi-purpose grant, he was promised their votes. That proved to be enough to get the legislation through the House.

When the bill moved to the Senate, it was again stalled. Several days passed before the Senate considered the bill, and several members hoped to offer amendments. Offering amendments at this late stage, however, would have unsettled the delicate balance arrived at in the House. Eventually the Senate approved the bill by a vote of 61-39. And during the signing ceremony, the president signaled the bipartisanship of the vote by inviting the Republicans who had negotiated with him to stand with him as the bill became law.

SUMMARY

Laws that affect all the citizens of the nation are made by the U.S. Congress, which derives its authority from Article I of the Constitution. Powers which were not given to Congress by the Constitution are reserved to the states, but over the years Congressional power has been greatly expanded. The lawmaking process at the state and federal levels is essentially the same, but is much more complicated at the federal level and is more time consuming than in most state legislatures. Each state, regardless of population, has two senators, but the number of House members varies according to each state's population. This compromise, agreed to in 1787 by delegates to the Constitutional Convention, allows the less populous states an equal voice in at least one of the nation's legislative chambers and helps to prevent the dominance of legislative matters by large states.

CHAPTER 11

Local Government

Local governments are the most numerous governmental units in the United States. There are 83,000 throughout the nation. Their authority is derived from laws enacted by state legislatures or from state constitutions. Local governments come in a variety of forms and provide a variety of services to residents of communities in every state and in the District of Columbia.

Although the focus of this book is on the lawmaking process at the state and federal levels, it is important to remember that many of the ordinances (laws), resolutions, rules, and regulations that affect everyday life are made at the local level. And because local government in all its forms—cities, towns, counties, school districts, special districts—is closer to individuals than the legislators in a state capitol or the legislators at the U.S. Capitol in Washington, D.C., it is often easier to make one's voice heard at the local level of government.

In the United States there are 83,000 units of local government. The organization of these units, and their powers and responsibilities, vary widely from state to state. Some county and city governments, for example, have the authority to make laws—usually referred to as ordinances or resolutions.

The relationship between state and local governments is similar to that between the federal government and the states. To understand the state-local government relationship you need to review the connections between the three levels of government—federal, state, and local—that were discussed earlier.

- The U.S. Constitution is the foundation for our system of government. It is from the Constitution, ratified originally by the 13 states that existed at its inception and acknowledged by each state that has entered the Union since then, that Congress derives its powers to make laws affecting all 50 states.
- The U.S. Constitution granted specific powers to the federal government and said that all powers that were not expressly granted to the federal government were reserved to the individual states. There was no mention of local governments in the U.S. Constitution; the delegation of powers was to the states, not to local government.
- Individual states also have their own constitutions. It is from the state constitution that the legislature derives its power to make laws for that particular state, including laws relating to the establishment and authority of local governments. In addition to being created as a result of legislative action, some local governments may also be established by the state constitution.

There are a variety of local governments in the 50 states. The basic types are counties and municipalities, which include cities, towns or townships, special districts, and school districts.

COUNTIES

Historically, counties were seen as a subdivision of state government, established for the basic purpose of administering state programs at the local level. Now, however, counties are traditionally granted powers necessary to provide services needed or demanded by residents in unincorporated areas.

In colonial times, county governments of England's colonies in America were known as "shires," the term used in England for local government units that resemble counties. In the colonies, shires eventually came to be known as counties. The first county was established in Virginia, and subsequently, counties became the major unit of local government in the southern and western states.

Today, there are 3,072 counties in the United States, according to the National Association of Counties. The number of counties in any given state depends, at least to some extent, on the geographic size of the state. Texas has 254 counties; Delaware, 3. The average is about 60 per state. In two states, Connecticut and Rhode Island, there are geographic areas designated as counties (eight in Connecticut; five in Rhode Island), but they have no governmental functions or structure and are not considered to be units of local government. In Connecticut, county government was abolished in 1960, but the former county boundaries were retained for the election of county sheriffs and for judicial purposes.

Louisiana's local governments that are the equivalent of counties are called "parishes;" and in Alaska, they are known as "boroughs."

County governments are defined by the U.S. Bureau of the Census as: "Organized local governments authorized in state constitutions and statutes and established to provide general government." The general government services they provide most often include law enforcement, correctional facilities (jails), construction and maintenance of roads, planning and zoning, health and welfare (which may include hospitals), and sanitary land fills. Other general government services that benefit the residents of a county may include the control of fireworks, animal control, issues relating to graffiti problems, noise control, and a judicial system to enforce county laws. Given the existence of more than 3,000 counties, however, there are exceptions to every generalization one could make about county government.

For example, the elected governing body—the county equivalent of the state legislature—goes by a variety of names. In a majority of states, the governing body is known as the Board of County Commissioners. In some states, it is the Board of Supervisors, and in others, it is known as the County Council. Those are the most frequently used terms. But there are a number of exceptions, including: Board of Chosen Freeholders (New Jersey); County Court (Missouri); Commissioners' Court (Texas); County Legislative Body (Tennessee); County Legislature, Board of Representatives, Legislative Board, and Board of Legislators (all in New York); Quorum or Levying Court (Arkansas); Fiscal Court (Kentucky); and Police Jury, Parish Council, and Commission Council (all in Louisiana). The legislative bodies, no matter what they are called, usually consist of three to five elected officials who vote on proposed ordinances.

At the county level, county governing bodies are the legislative bodies that have the authority to enact legislation dealing with the geographic areas for which they are responsible. The authority of most county governing boards to enact legislation is limited by the state constitution or by the state statutes, or both. Usually, county governing bodies must go to the state legislature for the authority to pass ordinances or resolutions, terms for laws enacted by local government.

For example, one of the legislators we followed in an earlier chapter, Senator Brian Caucus, sponsored legislation (Senate Bill 21) "Concerning the Power of Counties to Adopt Ordinances Relating to Juvenile Activities." The senator's bill, which was enacted, authorized county commissioners to adopt ordinances imposing curfews and punishing juveniles for loitering and producing graffiti. The bill was necessary because, in Senator Caucus's state, county governing bodies have the authority to pass laws of local concern (ordinances) only when they have been granted that authority by the state legislature.

In many states, counties and cities have an opportunity to be relatively independent of the legislature by adopting home-rule charters. Simply defined, home rule means self-government. It gives local governments some measure of independence from legislative control over the organization and operation of government activities at the local level. In states where it is permitted, the citizens of a county or a municipality can vote on the adoption of a charter, something similar to a constitution, which establishes the form of local government and the authority of the governing body. Home-rule counties and cities have the power to make laws governing local affairs, without having to go to the state legislature for specific authority. The bill that Senator Brian Caucus sponsored to allow counties to pass legislation concerning curfews, loitering, and graffiti is an example of one necessary for counties without home rule.

Cities have taken advantage of home rule much more frequently than counties. While there are numerous home-rule cities, there are only about 150 counties that have formally drawn up and adopted home-rule charters, including several consolidated city-county governments (according to a survey by Tanis Salant of the University of Arizona). Hundreds of other counties, however, have opted for increased statutory authorization for local powers, which often is more limited than a home-rule charter.

MUNICIPALITIES

Municipalities and towns provide general government for a specific concentration of population in a defined area. Like counties, cities have no powers except those granted to them by the state constitution, the state legislature, or both, which includes home-rule powers. Home-rule municipalities differ from statutory municipalities as defined by the origin of their powers, that is, home-rule cities and towns adopt, by a vote of their residents, their own "charter," which then governs services, taxes, fees, revenues, and usually the judicial system for enforcement. Statutory cities and towns derive their powers from state statutes and tailor them to meet the needs of residents by adopting ordinances relating to specific subjects.

However, neither counties nor municipalities can adopt a home-rule charter that is in conflict with the U.S. or state constitution, or state statutes that specifically exempt or prohibit local control because of state-wide concern.

Local governments use the words "ordinance" and "resolution" to define the proposals for law which the governing body adopts. Once adopted, each has the full force and effect of law and is subject to judicial review when contested.

There are several forms of city government, usually identified as the "weak mayor-council" plan, the "strong mayor-council" plan, and the "council-manager" plan. In all three forms, the city council, or legislative body, consists of elected officials. The differences are that in the weak mayor plan, the mayor is usually selected from among the elected council members to preside over council meetings but has no authority beyond that of other members of the city council. The council usually approves appointments, determines administrative functions, and adopts the budget.

In the strong mayor plan, the mayor is directly elected by the voters and exercises broad powers over the budget, as well as the power to appoint and remove appointed city officials. The mayor in such a plan usually presides at meetings but often does not have a vote except to break a tie. In some strong mayor systems, the mayor heads the executive branch of the municipality, similar to the governor of a state. In home-rule municipalities, the mayor's power and duties usually are stated in the charter.

In home-rule municipalities, the laws enacted by the city council are called ordinances. Council members may sponsor legislation, hold public hearings, and propose and adopt amendments before a final vote on the ordinance is taken. Cities without home-rule have much less power—their authority is limited to specific grants of power from the state. Municipalities without home-rule—those that derive their powers from the state statutes—are limited to specific grants of power from the state law, but do follow the same process as outlined above before a final vote is taken on proposed ordinances.

TOWNS AND TOWNSHIPS

These are forms of local government found primarily in New England (towns) and in northeastern and midwestern states (townships).

In colonial times, New England town meetings, attended by all the citizens of a town, village, and the surrounding countryside, were held to decide matters affecting the town government and to elect "selectmen" to oversee the town's affairs during the coming year. Today, however, as David Saffell explains in *State and Local Government*, "voters choose a large number of citizens (around 100) to attend the town meeting and represent their views."

Townships and towns are more numerous than cities and counties—there are about 16,000 town and township governments in 20 states. Towns differ from cities in that they usually serve a smaller, more rural population and consist of smaller, less densely populated areas requiring less sophisticated services. They derive their powers from state statutes and, in some states, may become home-rule towns authorized to adopt their own charter. Sometimes, a town is defined by a specific population, that is, 2,000 people and under is a town; a population over 2,000 is a city. State statutes usually authorize limited powers to a town to provide necessary public services such as zoning, fire protection, and water and sanitation services. Public transportation is not usually needed by town residents, and often road construction and maintenance, jails, and even law enforcement can be contracted for from the county. Services such as health and welfare, jails, and hospitals are provided by the county government. In some states, towns may opt for home-rule, the same as cities and counties.

SCHOOL DISTRICTS

Local governments with the highest visibility are the nation's 15,212 school districts. Public school districts are created by the state legislature, which may also have the power to consolidate existing districts. Through the appropriation process, state legislatures provide some of the funding needed for the operation of school districts. You may recall that one of the bills we followed through the legislative process earlier was Senate Bill 155, which called for a supplemental state appropriation for public schools.

The amount of state support varies, from highs of 90 percent of school budgets in Hawaii, 73 percent in New Mexico, and 71 percent in Washington state to lows of 8 percent in New Hampshire, 26 percent in Michigan, and 27 percent in South Dakota. The median state support for the 1991–

92 school year was 43 percent. School districts get the additional money they need from local property taxes, except in Michigan, where the state legislature abolished the property tax as a source of revenue for schools. Abolishing the property tax for schools meant that other sources of revenue would be necessary to provide state money for public schools. The other revenue sources that Michigan voters approved included tripling the cigarette tax, raising the sales tax from 4 cents to 6 cents, and imposing a 0.75 percent real estate transfer tax.

Whatever the source of the money, it is the local school board that determines how it is spent. Generally, school board members are elected and have the power to make decisions affecting the operation of a particular district. The authority of school boards normally includes the power to hire teachers and other employees and to make decisions regarding the curriculum, budgeting, and all other matters relevant to the operation of the public schools for which a board is responsible. Elected school boards are, in effect, the legislative body for a specific district. They do not have free reign, however, because they must operate within the powers granted to them by the state legislature and within legislation concerning public schools that the state legislature enacts.

Most of the nation's school districts are independent, that is, the elected school boards that govern them have the authority to determine the tax levy necessary to produce the money—beyond that supplied by the state—to operate the local school system and to make other decisions regarding the public schools within their jurisdiction. There are, however, more than 1,000 dependent districts whose monetary needs are provided by the governments they serve and whose budgets are subject to review and change by those governments. Dependent school districts usually have elected governing bodies responsible for administering the schools.

SPECIAL DISTRICTS

Special districts are the most numerous local governments—there are about 30,000 in the 50 states and the District of Columbia—and their function is to provide municipal services to a defined geographical area. Special districts are created by a vote of the residents the district will serve. The vote to form a special district will also define specific services to be provided and the source of revenue to provide funds for the district's operations. Special districts usually provide service to unincorporated areas within a county but may include cities and towns, and may also cross county boundaries.

As with other local governments, special districts derive their authority from laws passed by the state legislature or from the state constitution, usually from powers delegated to them by the legislature. Special districts are governed by a board of directors, who may be elected or appointed for specific terms.

Special districts provide a wide variety of services such as fire protection, water supply, sewerage systems, drainage and flood control, soil and water conservation, parks and recreation, housing and community development, cemeteries, hospitals, libraries, and airports and other transportation facilities.

Special districts range from autonomous units of local government to "sub-governments" of a county, depending on state law. An example of an autonomous or independent special district would be one formed to provide services to new growth or development on land that has no roads or services, or to an area where homes and businesses are using wells for water and septic tanks for sewage. In the latter example, should the well water become polluted and require treatment, a water and sanitation district could be formed to provide such services.

In sparsely populated areas, the residents may choose to band together to form a fire district for fire protection services, and perhaps emergency medical services. In any case, the procedures to create a special district are set forth in state statutes, which vary considerably from state to state.

SUMMARY

In states having counties, everyone lives within a county. Services provided by counties range from law enforcement and planning and zoning to services specifically requested by citizens. Counties normally do not provide municipal-type services that are not practical in sparsely-populated areas. For example, it is not economically feasible to run water or sewer lines from house to house when they are miles apart.

Municipal government varies a great deal. Some examples include city-county governments such as Denver, Colorado, and Dade County, Florida, where traditional county government services are combined with municipal services under one governing body and one charter. Most municipalities serving a large land area and high density population will have adopted a home-rule charter for governance purposes and will include a judicial system to enforce municipal ordinances.

Towns or townships usually are smaller, more rural population centers. In some states, they may also be allowed to adopt a home-rule charter, and usually do not have a separate judicial system.

Special districts normally are strong, locally controlled entities with an elected governing body, and can vary from small geographic areas to very large, densely populated areas. Special districts fill the need for providing services primarily in unincorporated areas, but may also include entire municipalities. Special district services usually include all municipal-type services except police powers and zoning.

CHAPTER 12

Citizens

Making laws is generally the responsibility of elected officials, whether at the national, state, or local level. In 24 states, however, citizens themselves may propose laws and, in some states, amendments to the state constitution through the initiative process. In some states, citizens may also have the power to call for a statewide vote to approve or reject laws enacted by the legislature. In others, citizens have the authority to recall elected officials before the end of their term of office. These three direct democracy procedures—the initiative, the referendum, and the recall—are the subject of the final chapter.

In a majority of the states (26), laws can be made only by members of the state legislature who are elected to represent the citizens of a particular district. That is the way our representative system of government is structured. It would be impossible for all the citizens of the United States (260 million people spread across thousands of miles), of a state (from California's 31 million residents to Wyoming's 465,000), a county, a municipality, or any other unit of local government to meet at any point in time at a single location to make the laws that govern them.

It was not always that way. In earlier times, when there were fewer people, it was possible for the citizens of a town to meet and vote on laws of a local jurisdiction, which was the custom in New England's town meetings.

In our time, at least in the United States, it is no longer possible to hold town meetings—or any variation of town meetings—that give each citizen an opportunity to vote on proposed laws.

There are procedures in 24 states, however, that provide citizens an opportunity to have a direct voice in making laws, amending the state constitution, approving or rejecting laws passed by the state legislature, and removing elected officials from office. In these states, citizens can be political activists in the truest since of that phrase. Instead of staging sign-carrying protests, they can make a difference through direct democracy.

There are three methods of direct democracy: the **initiative**, the **referendum**, and **recall**.

- The initiative enables citizens to bypass the legislature by placing proposed statutes and, in some states, constitutional amendments directly on the ballot to be voted on by all the citizens at a regular election.
- The referendum provides for a popular vote on laws that have been passed by the legislature.
- The recall allows citizens to remove elected officials from office before the end of an official's term of office.

In the United States, the initiative, referendum, and recall movement can be traced directly to the populist and progressive eras of the late nineteenth and early twentieth centuries when state governments were perceived to be controlled by special interests such as railroads, banks, and land speculators. Direct democracy, especially the initiative, was seen as a way to give citizens an opportunity to make laws that the legislature refused to consider because of the influence of special interests, or on which the legislature was unable to reach agreement.

THE INITIATIVE

The political definition of "initiative" is "the right of a group of citizens to introduce a matter for legislation either to the legislature or directly to the voters," and "the procedure by which such matters are introduced, usually a petition signed by a specified percentage of the voters."

The first state to adopt the initiative was South Dakota, in 1898. Since then, 23 other states have amended their constitutions to include the initiative process (see Table 11.1)

There are two types of initiatives, direct and indirect. In the direct process, proposals that qualify go directly on the ballot. In the indirect

process, they are submitted to the legislature, which has an opportunity to act on the
proposed legislation. In some states, the legislature may amend the proposal or enact a
substitute measure. Other states prohibit
the legislature from changing the proposed
law. In the indirect process, the legislature
is given various lengths of time to act on an
initiative and—depending on the state—
the initiative question goes on the ballot if
the legislature rejects it, submits a different
proposal, or takes no action. In any event, a
legislature must consider indirect initiatives
that have been submitted, even though that
consideration may result in the legislature
taking no formal action on the proposed
initiative.

No two states have exactly the same requirements for qualifying initiative questions to be placed on the ballot or sent to
the legislature. In general, however, the process includes the following steps:

TABLE 11.1	
INITIATIVE STATES	
State	**Year Initiative Adopted**
Alaska	1959 **
Arizona	1910
Arkansas	1909
California	1911
Colorado	1910
Florida	1972 *
Idaho	1912 **
Illinois	1970 *
Maine	1908 **
Massachusetts	1918
Michigan	1908
Mississippi	1992 *
Missouri	1906
Montana	1904
Nebraska	1912
Nevada	1904
North Dakota	1914
Ohio	1912
Oklahoma	1907
Oregon	1902
South Dakota	1898
Utah	1900 **
Washington	1912 **
Wyoming	1968 **

*Applies only to constitutional
  amendments.
**Applies only to statutes.

1. Preliminary filing of a proposed peti-
   tion with a state official (usually the secretary of state);
2. Review of the petition to make sure that it conforms with requirements set forth in the state statutes and, in several states, a review of
   the language of the proposal;
3. Preparation of a ballot title and a summary of the proposed law or
   constitutional amendment. In general, ballot titles summarize the
   specific provisions of an initiative.

When all those requirements have been met, initiative petitions must
be circulated throughout the state to obtain the required number of
individual signatures of registered voters. The number of signatures that
backers of an initiative must get varies from state to state but is usually
based on a percentage of the votes cast for a statewide office in the
preceding general election. When the supporters of an initiative have
enough signatures, the initiative is submitted to the state elections official,
who must verify the number of signatures. If enough valid signatures are

obtained, the question proposed by the initiative is placed on the ballot or, in states with the indirect process, sent to the legislature.

Central to the process, obviously, is getting the required number of signatures. Early advocates of the initiative viewed circulating petitions among registered voters as a demonstration of widespread public support for a proposed law or constitutional amendment. They expected the petitions to be circulated by informed citizens who were concerned about public policy questions not being addressed by the legislature.

While that may still be the case in some instances, many petition drives now are highly organized, professional campaigns, employing paid circulators. Collecting the required number of signatures is not an easy job. In recent years in California, for example, supporters of an initiative petition had to have 433,269 signatures of registered voters to get a statutory proposal on the ballot and 693,230 signatures to get a constitutional amendment on the ballot. And to be sure that an initiative will qualify, backers of an initiative often have to gather perhaps a third more signatures than the required number because many people who sign petitions are not registered voters and their signatures will be thrown out in the final count. Even in less populous states like Colorado, 49,279 valid signatures were recently needed to place a proposal on the ballot.

What that has come to mean is that the essential ingredient for getting a proposed law or constitutional amendment on the ballot is money. In California, for example, it has been estimated that $1 million spent on a petition drive will guarantee an initiative a place on the ballot. Only two initiative campaigns in California have spent more than $500,000 and not qualified.

Individual citizens, by volunteering to circulate petitions, can still play an active role in having a direct voice in government. Even in initiative, referendum, and recall drives that employ paid circulators, volunteers are a necessary part of a campaign.

Once an initiative question is on the ballot, the general requirement for passage is a majority vote. Nebraska, Massachusetts, and Mississippi, however, are exceptions. Those states require a majority, provided the votes cast on the initiative equal a percentage of the total votes cast in the election (35 percent in Nebraska, 30 percent in Massachusetts, and 40 percent in Mississippi). For example, if 700,000 votes were cast in a general election in Mississippi, there would have to be 280,000 votes cast on the initiative question and the initiative proposal would have to receive at least 140,001 votes to pass. For an initiative to pass in Wyoming it must receive votes "in an amount in excess of 50 percent of those voting in the general election." In Nevada, an initiated constitutional amendment must receive a majority vote in two successive general elections.

Initiatives can propose laws or constitutional amendments (or both in some states) on nearly any subject, although there are some restrictions. Most of the 24 initiative states, for example, prohibit proposals that would appropriate money from the state treasury. Examples of other prohibitions on the subject matter of initiatives include laws relating to religion, the judiciary, and local or special legislation. In some states, initiatives must relate to only one subject.

Initiatives approved by the voters in Arizona, California, and Colorado in recent elections are examples of the wide variety of subject matter addressed through direct citizen action.

Proposition 107, Arizona

Proposition 107, an amendment to the Arizona state constitution that limits the terms of members of Congress from Arizona, as well as the terms of state senators, state representatives, and other elected state officials, was on the ballot in 1992. It was approved by Arizona voters, but the U.S. Supreme Court ruled, in a 1995 decision, that an Arkansas initiative that limited the terms of members of Congress was unconstitutional, thus nullifying a portion of the Arizona initiative; when the U.S. Supreme Court says that a limit on the number of terms of members of Congress from Arkansas violates the U.S. Constitution, it follows that no other state can limit the terms of U.S. senators or representatives.

The full text of the Arizona initiative follows.

Proposition 107
Arizona, 1992
(The initiative was passed)
OFFICIAL TITLE
AN INITIATIVE MEASURE

PROPOSING AMENDMENTS TO THE CONSTITUTION OF ARIZONA TO KEEP THE NAMES OF SENATORS FROM ARIZONA TO THE UNITED STATES SENATE WHO ARE COMPLETING TWO CONSECUTIVE TERMS (12 YEARS) AND REPRESENTATIVES FROM ARIZONA TO THE UNITED STATES HOUSE OF REPRESENTATIVES WHO ARE COMPLETING THREE CONSECUTIVE TERMS (6 YEARS) FROM BEING PRINTED ON THE BALLOT BY AMENDING ARTICLE VII TO ADD SECTION 18; TO LIMIT THE TERMS OF STATE SENA-TORS AND REPRESENTATIVES TO FOUR CONSECUTIVE TERMS (8 YEARS)

BY AMENDING ARTICLE IV, PART 2, SECTION 21; TO LIMIT THE TERMS OF OFFICE OF MEMBERS OF THE ARIZONA EXECUTIVE DEPARTMENT TO TWO CONSECUTIVE TERMS (8 YEARS) BY AMENDING ARTICLE V. SECTION 1(A); TO DELETE ARTICLE V, SECTION 10, PERTAINING TO THE LIMITATION OF TERMS OF THE STATE TREASURER, AS IT IS SUPERSEDED BY THE AMENDMENT PROPOSED BY THIS INITIATIVE MEASURE; TO LIMIT THE TERMS OF OFFICE OF MEMBERS OF THE CORPORATION COMMISSION TO ONE CONSECUTIVE TERM (6 YEARS) BY AMENDING ARTICLE XV; AND TO LIMIT THE TERMS OF OFFICE OF THE STATE MINE INSPECTOR TO FOUR CONSECUTIVE TERMS (8 YEARS) BY AMENDING ARTICLE XIX. Underlining in the text indicates additions to the present provisions. Strike through indicates deletions to the present provisions.

TEXT OF PROPOSED AMENDMENT

Be it enacted by the People of the Senate of Arizona: The following amendments to the Constitution of the State of Arizona, amending Article VII to add § 18, amending Article IV, part 2, § 21 and Article V, §1 A, deleting Article V, § 10, amending Article XV § 1 and amending Article XIX are proposed to become valid when approved by a majority of the qualified electors voting thereon and on proclamation of the governor:

§ 1. THE CONSTITUTION OF THE STATE OF ARIZONA IS AMENDED BY ADDING ARTICLE VII SECTION 18.

Article VII. Section 18.

§ 18.**Term limits on ballot appearances in congressional elections**.

Section 18.   The name of any candidate for United States Senator from Arizona shall not appear on the ballot if by the end of the current term of office, the candidate will have served (or but for resignation would have served) in that office for two consecutive terms, and the name of a candidate for United States Representative from Arizona shall not appear on the ballot if by the end of the current term of office the candidate will have served (or but for resignation would have served) in that office for three consecutive terms. Terms are considered consecutive unless they are at least one full term apart. Any person appointed or elected to fill a vacancy in the United States Congress who serves at least one half of a term of office shall be considered to have served a term in that office for purposes of this section. For purposes of this section terms beginning before January 1, 1993 shall not be considered.

§ 2. THE CONSTITUTION OF THE STATE OF ARIZONA IS AMENDED BY AMENDING ARTICLE IV, PART 2, SECTION 21.

Article IV. Part 2. Section 21.

§ 21.   **Term limits of members of state legislature.**

Section 21. The members of the first Legislature shall hold office until the first Monday in January, 1913. The terms of office of the members of succeeding Legislatures shall be two years. No state Senator shall serve more than four consecutive terms in that office nor shall any state Representative serve more than four consecutive terms in that office. This limitation on the number of terms of consecutive service shall apply to terms of office beginning on or after January 1, 1993. No Legislator, after serving the maximum number of terms which shall include any part of a term served, may serve in the same office until he has been out of office for no less than one full term.

§ 3. THE CONSTITUTION OF THE STATE OF ARIZONA IS AMENDED BY AMENDING ARTICLE V, SECTION 1 (A).

Article V, Section 1.

§ 1. **Term limits** on Executive department; **and** state officers; **terms lengths;** election; residence and office at seat of government; duties.

Section 1. A. The executive department shall consist of the governor, secretary of state, state treasurer, attorney general, and superintendent of public instruction, each of whom shall hold office for a term of four years beginning on the first Monday of January, 1971 next after the regular general election in 1970. No member of the executive department shall hold that office for more than two consecutive terms. This limitation on the number of terms of consecutive service shall apply to terms of office beginning on or after January 1, 1993. No member of the executive department after serving the maximum number of terms which shall include any part of a term served may serve in the same office until out of office for no less than one full term.

§ 4. THE CONSTITUTION OF THE STATE OF ARIZONA IS AMENDED BY DELETING ARTICLE V, SECTION 10. SECTIONS 11, 12 AND 13 OF ARTICLE V SHALL BE RENUMBERED TO PROVIDE FOR CONSECUTIVE NUMBERING AFTER THE DELETION OF PRESENT SECTION 10.

Article V, Section 10.

§ 10. Ineligibility of state treasurer to succeed himself.

Section 10. No person shall be eligible to succeed himself to the office of State Treasurer for the succeeding two years after the expiration of the term for which he shall have been elected.

§ 5. THE CONSTITUTION OF THE STATE OF ARIZONA IS AMENDED BY ADDING ARTICLE XV, SECTION 1 (A).

Article XV, Section 1.

§ 1. Term limits on Corporation Commission; Composition; election; term of office; office and residence; vacancies; qualifications.

Section 1. A. No member of the Corporation Commission shall hold that office for more than one consecutive term. No Corporation Commissioner after serving that term may serve in that office until out of office for one full term. Any person who serves one half or more of a term shall be considered to have served one term for purposes of this section. This limitation shall apply to terms of office beginning on or after January 1, 1993.

§ 6. THE CONSTITUTION OF THE STATE OF ARIZONA IS AMENDED BY AMENDING ARTICLE XIX.

Article XIX.

The office of Mine Inspector is hereby established. The Legislature, at its first session, shall enact laws to regulate the operation and equipment of all mines in the State as to provide for the health and safety of workers therein and in connection therewith, and fixing the duties of said office. Upon approval of such laws by the Governor, the Governor, with the advice and consent of the Senate, shall forthwith appoint a Mine Inspector, who shall serve until his successor shall have been elected at the first general election thereafter and shall qualify. Said successor and all subsequent incumbents of said office shall be elected at general elections, and shall serve for a term of two years. No Mine Inspector shall serve more than four consecutive terms in the office. No Mine Inspector after serving the maximum number of terms, which shall include any part of a term served, may serve in the same office until out of office for no less than one full term. This limitation on the number of terms of consecutive service shall apply to terms of office beginning on or after January 1, 1993.

§ 7. SEVERABILITY. IF ANY PROVISION OF THIS INITIATIVE OR ITS APPLICATION TO ANY PERSON OR CIRCUMSTANCE IS HELD INVALID, THE INVALIDITY DOES NOT AFFECT OTHER PROVISIONS OR APPLICATIONS OF THE ACT THAT CAN BE GIVEN EFFECT WITHOUT THE INVALID PROVISION OR APPLICATION, AND TO THIS END THE PROVISIONS OF THIS ACT ARE SEVERABLE.

Proposition 187, California

This statutory initiative, the purpose of which was to deny public education, nonemergency health care, and public social services to illegal immigrants, qualified for the ballot in 1994 and passed. The vote was 5,063,537 in favor and 3,529,432 against. During the 1994 election campaign it became known as the "Save our State" initiative.

Because Mexico and California share a common border, many citizens of Mexico cross the border illegally to work in California, where wages are higher. While they are living and working in California, even though they are still citizens of Mexico and living in the U.S. illegally, California provides, at state expense, a variety of governmental services, including schools, health services, and public social services. Supporters of the initiative estimated the state cost of educational services alone for illegal immigrants at about $1.7 billion a year. They argued that the state of California should not be burdened with the cost of education, and other public services, for illegal immigrants and their families.

Backers of the initiative also argued that passage of the measure would lead to more deportations of illegal immigrants and to lower public service costs for citizens and legal residents.

Opponents maintained that passage of Prop 187 would cause more problems than it solved, especially in the area of enforcing its terms. They also argued that many of its provisions are contrary to state and federal laws, court decisions, and the U.S. Constitution.

After Proposition 187 passed, it was challenged in the courts and is awaiting a U.S. Supreme Court decision on the constitutionality of its provisions.

Amendment 2, Colorado

Another controversial initiative is Colorado's Amendment 2, approved by the voters in 1992. It amended the state constitution to prohibit the state, state agencies, cities, school districts, and other political subdivisions from adopting or enforcing laws or policies entitling anyone to claim discrimination, protected status, minority status, or quota preferences based on homosexual, lesbian, or bisexual relationships.

Three Colorado cities—Aspen, Boulder, and Denver—had local ordinances that protected individuals from job and housing discrimination based on sexual orientation. Amendment 2 struck down those local laws.

Supporters of Amendment 2 contend that homosexuals should not be given special status because of their sexual orientation. Opponents argue that the real issue involves the civil rights of individuals. The federal Civil

---

Amendment 2—Colorado

"No Protected Status Based on Homosexual, Lesbian, or Bisexual Orientation. Neither the State of Colorado, through any of its branches or departments, nor any of its agencies, political subdivisions, municipalities or school districts, shall enact, adopt or enforce any statute, regulation, ordinance or policy whereby homosexual, lesbian or bisexual orientation, conduct, practices or relationships shall constitute or otherwise be the basis of or entitle any person or class of persons to have or claim any minority status, quota preference, protected status or claim of discrimination. This section of the Constitution shall be in all respects self-executing."

Colorado voters passed Amendment 2 by a vote of 53.4 percent to 46.6 percent.

Rights Act of 1964 and laws enacted by states and local governments since that time have prohibited discrimination in employment, housing, access to public accommodations, and other areas involving civil rights. Amendment 2, its opponents say, identifies one area—discrimination based on sexual relationships—in which civil rights laws could *not* be enacted by state or local governments.

As with California's Proposition 187, Amendment 2 has been challenged. Since the legal arguments involved are complicated, a decision on the constitutionality of Amendment 2 has yet to be made by the U.S. Supreme Court.

All initiatives approved by the voters are not challenged in the courts; in fact, most are not. And all those that do go to the courts are not declared unconstitutional. The California and Colorado initiatives were both highly controversial issues which were expected to face challenges from opponents in the event that they passed.

The same thing could be said concerning laws enacted by a legislature—controversial legislation passed by any state legislature may be challenged on constitutional grounds.

THE REFERENDUM

Of the three devices of direct democracy—the initiative, the referendum, and recall of elected officials—the referendum is the most confusing. The confusion may arise because a vote on any question is a referendum. Using that definition, there are several varieties of statewide, as well as local, referenda.

The most common statewide referendum is a vote on a constitutional amendment proposed by the legislature. In every state, except Delaware, constitutional amendments proposed by the legislature must be approved by the voters. In Delaware, constitutional amendments require a two-thirds vote by two successive legislatures rather than being submitted to the voters. In 18 states, amendments also may be proposed by citizens using the initiative process described above (see Table 11.1).

In addition to constitutional amendments, other types of referenda (ballot questions) that the legislature can propose include advisory questions, statutes, and the issuance of state bonds.

In many states, various units of local government may also have the authority to place referenda on the ballot to be voted on by the citizens residing within the boundaries of a local government unit. Examples of these local governments would include city councils, county commissions, and school boards. Referenda placed on the ballot by local governments most frequently involve questions relating to taxes or the issuance of bonds.

Another form of the referendum, and the subject of the rest of this discussion, is the process that provides for a citizen-initiated popular vote on laws that have been enacted by the legislature. For example, if a state legislature enacted a law requiring all cars to pass an emissions test and there were citizens who disagreed with this legislation, they could force a popular vote on the question of approving or rejecting the emissions test law through a referendum

Although this type of referendum—sometimes called the "popular referendum"—is less frequently used than the initiative, it is available to citizens in 25 states (see box below).

As with other forms of direct democracy, the popular referendum process varies from state to state, but, generally, it includes these steps:

1. A request for permission to circulate a petition filed with a specified state official—usually the secretary of state;
2. Circulation of the petition to gather the required number of signatures and filing of the completed petition with the state elections officer;
3. Certification of the petition for the ballot when the required number of valid signatures are verified;
4. A vote on the question at the next general election, although a few states provide for special elections.

In all states, except North Dakota, the number of signatures required is determined by a percentage of the votes cast in a preceding statewide election, usually for governor. The percentages vary from a low of 2 percent of the total population in North Dakota to 15 percent of the total votes in the last general election in Wyoming. The most common requirements range from 3 percent to 6 percent of the total votes in a preceding election; 16 of the 25 popular referendum states are in this category.

Referendum petitions must be filed within a relatively short time

Popular Referendum States	
Alaska	Montana
Arizona	Nebraska
Arkansas	Nevada
California	New Mexico
Colorado	North Dakota
Idaho	Ohio
Illinois	Oklahoma
Kentucky	Oregon
Maine	South Dakota
Maryland	Utah
Massachusetts	Washington
Michigan	Wyoming
Missouri	

period—in most states, within 90 days after the close of the legislative session during which the law in question was enacted. When valid petitions have been filed, the legislation being challenged does not take effect, pending the result of the popular vote. In each of the 25 referendum states, a majority of the popular vote is necessary to approve the legislation being questioned.

In addition to a brief period of time to gather signatures, restrictions on laws subject to a popular referendum discourage its use. Arkansas, Idaho, and Nevada are the only states with no restrictions on laws that may be challenged. Generally, statutes enacted by the legislature that are not subject to popular referendum are those involving revenue, taxation, and appropriations.

In 13 states, there is another catch as well: Laws that are "necessary for the immediate preservation of the public peace, health, and safety" are exempt from the popular referendum process. In Colorado, where every bill enacted by the legislature routinely includes such a "safety clause," the phrase precludes popular referendums even though the state's constitution and statutes provide for the process. Some of the bills used as examples in previous chapters include a safety clause that would prohibit a popular referendum on the bill.

Massachusetts, on the other hand, makes it more difficult for the legislature to exempt "emergency" or "safety clause" statutes from a referendum. In that state, laws that are "necessary for the immediate preservation of the public peace, health, safety or convenience" must contain a preamble setting forth the facts constituting the emergency. This preamble must then be adopted by a two-thirds vote in each chamber. Massachusetts prohibits referendums on measures relating to religion, judges, and the judiciary.

Utah citizens may not challenge statutes which are enacted by a two-thirds vote in each chamber. Illinois limits the popular referendum to questions of public policy that are advisory only and allows no more than three advisory public questions at any given election. Kentucky is not always counted among the referendum states because its provision for a popular referendum applies only to legislative acts classifying and providing for different levels of property taxation. The popular referendum has never been used in Kentucky.

Because the 25 popular referendum states, in fact, make it difficult to use, citizen activists have employed it much less frequently than the initiative.

THE RECALL

The recall procedure allows citizens to remove and replace a public official before the end of a term of office. Historically, recall has been used most frequently at the local level. By some estimates, three-fourths of recall elections are at the city council or school board level. If Megan McNally, for example, had felt strongly about it, she might have begun a recall drive for one or more members of the school board who were responsible for eliminating girls' basketball. She decided, instead, to lobby the state legislature for increased funding of public schools.

Recall differs from **impeachment,** another method of removing officials from office, in that it is a political device while impeachment is a legal process. Impeachment of a public official requires the House of a state legislature to level specific charges against an elected official, such as bribery or malfeasance in office. The Senate then acts as a jury. In most of the 17 states that have the recall process, specific reasons to recall an official are not required, and recall of an official is by a popular election.

There are 17 states that permit recall of state officials (see Figure 12.1). The District of Columbia also provides for recalls. So does Virginia, but it is usually not listed as a recall state because its process, while requiring

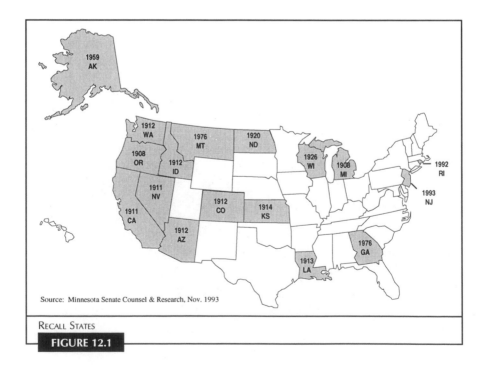

Source: Minnesota Senate Counsel & Research, Nov. 1993

RECALL STATES

FIGURE 12.1

citizen petitions as the first step, allows a recall trial rather than an election.

In 36 states recall elections may be held in local units of government such as cities, counties, school boards, and special districts. The recall device in the United States began, in fact, in a municipality—Los Angeles—in 1903. Michigan and Oregon, in 1908, were the first states to adopt recall procedures for state officials; and New Jersey and Rhode Island were the most recent states to adopt amendments to their state constitutions providing for the recall of state officials.

Supporters of the recall argue that it provides a method for citizens to retain control over elected officials who are not representing the best interests of their constituents or who are unresponsive or incompetent. These supporters believe that an elected representative is an agent, whose votes should reflect the wishes of a majority of his or her constituents.

Opponents of the recall maintain that it can lead to an excess of democracy. The threat of a recall election lessens the independence of elected officials, undermines the principle of electing good officials who will be given a chance to govern until the next election, and can lead to abuses by well-financed special interest groups.

Even though there are no reliable statistics, it is safe to say most recall elections occur at the local level. Local officials, such as members of a city council, county commission, or school board, make decisions that have a more direct and immediate effect on citizens than those made by elected officials who are further removed (state legislators and governors); therefore, citizens are more likely to organize recall efforts aimed at local, rather than state officials.

At the state level, where statistics are available, recalls have been singularly unsuccessful. In California, where 108 recall efforts were initiated between 1911 and 1995, only five qualified for the ballot. A state senator was recalled in 1913. In 1914, one senator was recalled and another survived a recall attempt. Not until 1994 was another state recall election held, and the senator involved in that attempt retained his office with 59 percent of the vote. A 1995 recall election of a California state representative, however, was successful, resulting in the representative's removal from office.

Recall efforts against two Michigan state senators in 1983 were successful, for the first time in that state's history. In Arizona, Governor Evan Mecham was the subject of a recall attempt in 1987. The recall election was never held, however, because he was impeached before the citizens of Arizona were able to cast their votes.

The recall process is similar to the initiative process in that citizen petitions are required. The number of signatures necessary to qualify a recall petition, however, is significantly higher than for initiatives. Signature requirements are based on a formula, usually a percentage of the vote in the last election for the office in question, although in some states the formula is based on the number of eligible voters or other variables. Whatever the formula, the signature requirements are high: 25 percent in nine states—Alaska, Arizona, Colorado, Michigan, Nevada, North Dakota, Oregon, Wisconsin, and New Jersey; 25 percent for statewide offices and 35 percent for legislators in Washington state; 33 percent in Louisiana; and 40 percent in Kansas. California's requirements are 12 percent for statewide offices; 20 percent for legislators and appeals court judges. Georgia requires 15 percent for statewide offices; 30 percent for all others. Idaho's requirement is 20 percent for all elected offices. Montana has the lowest number of required signatures, 10 percent for statewide officials and 15 percent for state district offices, such as state representatives and senators.

Specific reasons for recall are required in only four states: Alaska, Kansas, Montana, and Washington. Alaska's list of reasons for recall include incompetence, neglect of duty, and corruption; Kansas and Montana's include conviction for a felony and misconduct in office. The language in Michigan's constitution, however, is more typical of most states and acknowledges the political nature of many recall efforts: "The sufficiency of any statement of reasons or grounds (for recall of an elected official) shall be a political rather than a judicial question." What that means is that a citizen who may want to recall an elected official needs no specific legal reason, such as bribery, graft, corruption, or malfeasance in office, to attempt a recall effort.

When supporters of a recall have gathered enough signatures, a recall election is scheduled. In several states, the recall election is held simultaneously with an election for the official's successor. In this process, the first question on the ballot is whether the official should be recalled. Voters are then asked to vote for a candidate for the office. Votes on the candidates are tallied only if the vote on the first question—recall of the elected official—is positive. In other states, the first election involves only the question of recalling the official. If the vote is for recall, the office becomes vacant and is filled at a special election or "as prescribed by law," which in some states might be by appointment for the remainder of the term.

SUMMARY

In our representative form of government, laws are made by officials elected to represent their constituents. This is because it is impossible for all the citizens of the U.S. or of a state, a county, or a city to meet at one place at the same time in order to pass the laws that govern them.

In many of the 50 states, however, there are devices that give citizens an opportunity to have a direct voice in making laws, approving or rejecting laws that have been enacted by their representatives, and in removing elected officials from office.

These direct democracy procedures are the initiative, the referendum, and the recall. The process for using any of these devices varies from state to state. The critical element of the three direct democracy procedures involves gathering a specific number of signatures of registered voters in order to qualify a question—whether it is an initiative, a referendum, or a recall effort—for a place on the ballot.

Because of the number of signatures required to qualify initiative, referendum, or recall petitions for the ballot, it is difficult for an individual to mount a successful drive to place a proposed statute, a constitutional amendment, a referendum, or a question involving the recall of an elected official on the ballot. Many of these efforts now involve highly organized and professional campaigns. But there is still room for citizen activists who feel strongly enough about public policy questions to volunteer their time to these direct democracy campaigns.

PART

V

• • • • • • • • • •

Appendices

1. Vetoes and Veto Override

State	Amount	Other (b)	Days Allowed Governor to Consider Bill (a) During Session — Bill becomes law unless vetoed	Days Allowed Governor to Consider Bill (a) After Session — Bill becomes law unless vetoed	Days Allowed Governor to Consider Bill (a) After Session — Bill dies unless signed	Votes required in each house to pass bills or items over veto (c)
Alabama	Yes	Yes	6		10A	Majority elected
Alaska	Yes (d)	No	15	20P		2/3 elected (e)
Arizona	Yes	No	5	10A		2/3 elected
Arkansas	Yes	Yes	5	20A(f)		Majority elected
California	Yes (d)	No	12 (f,g)	(g)		2/3 elected
Colorado	Yes	Yes	10 (f)	30A (f)		2/3 elected
Connecticut	Yes	Yes	5	15P (f)		2/3 elected
Delaware	Yes	Yes	10		30A (f)	3/5 elected
Florida	Yes	Yes	7 (f)	15P (f)		2/3 elected
Georgia (h)	Yes	No	6 (f)	40A (f,i)		2/3 elected
Hawaii	Yes (d)	No	10 (j,k)	45A (j,k)	(k)	2/3 elected
Idaho	Yes	Yes	5	10A		2/3 elected
Illinois	Yes (d)	No	60 (f)	60P (f)		3/5 elected (e)
Indiana	No	No	7	7P(f)		Majority elected
Iowa	Yes	Yes	3	(l)	(l)	2/3 elected
Kansas	Yes	No	10 (f)	10P		2/3 elected
Kentucky	Yes	No	10	10A		Majority elected
Louisiana (h)	Yes	Yes	10 (f)	20P (f)		2/3 elected
Maine	No	No	10	(i)		2/3 present
Maryland (h)	Yes	Yes	6	30P(i)		3/5 elected
Massachusetts	Yes (d)	Yes	10		10P	2/3 present
Michigan	Yes (d)	Yes	14	(f)	14P(f)	2/3 elected and serving
Minnesota	Yes	No	3		14A	2/3 elected
Mississippi	Yes	Yes	5	15P(i)		2/3 elected
Missouri	Yes	No	15(f)	45P(f,i)		2/3 elected

Vetoes and Veto Override (continued)

State	Amount	Other (b)	Days Allowed Governor to Consider Bill (a)			Votes required in each house to pass bills or items over veto (c)
			During Session	After Session		
			Bill becomes law unless vetoed	Bill becomes law unless vetoed	Bill dies unless signed	
Montana	Yes	Yes	5(f)	25A(f)		2/3 present
Nebraska	Yes (m)	No	5	5A		3/5 elected
Nevada	No	No	5	10A		2/3 elected
New Hampshire	No	No	5		5P	2/3 elected
New Jersey	Yes (d)		No	45 (f,n)	(n)	2/3 elected (n)
New Mexico	Yes	No	3		20A	2/3 present
New York	Yes	No	10		30A	2/3 elected
North Carolina	(o)	(o)	(o)	(o)	(o)	(o)
North Dakota	Yes	Yes	3	15A		2/3 elected
Ohio	Yes	Yes	10	10A		3/5 elected
Oklahoma	Yes	Yes	5		15A	2/3 elected (e)
Oregon	Yes	Yes	5	(j)	30A (j)	2/3 present
Pennsylvania	Yes	Yes	10 (f)	30A (f)		2/3 elected
Rhode Island	No	No	6	10A (f)		3/5 present
South Carolina	Yes	Yes	5	(i)		2/3 present
South Dakota	Yes	Yes	5(f)	15A(f)		2/3 elected
Tennessee	Yes (d)		No	10	10A	Majority elected
Texas	Yes	No	10	20A		2/3 present
Utah	Yes	No	10	20A (f)		2/3 elected
Vermont	No	No	5		3A	2/3 present
Virginia	Yes	Yes	7	(f)		2/3 present (r)
Washington	Yes	Yes	5	20A	30A (f)	2/3 present
West Virginia	Yes (d)	Yes	5	15A (p)	60P	Majority elected (e)
Wisconsin	Yes	Yes	6			2/3 elected
Wyoming	Yes	Yes	3	15A (f)		2/3 elected

Sources: State constitutions and statutes.

Vetoes and Veto Override (continued)

Note: Some legislatures reconvene after normal session to consider bills vetoed by governor. *Connecticut*—if governor vetoes any bill, secretary of state must reconvene General Assembly on second Monday after the last day on which governor is either authorized to transmit or has transmitted every bill with his objections, whichever occurs first; General Assembly must adjourn sine die not later than three days after its reconvening. *Hawaii*—legislature may reconvene on 45th day after adjournment sine die, in special session, without call. *Louisiana*—legislature meets in a maximum five-day veto session on the 40th day after final adjournment. *Missouri*—if governor returns any bill on or after the fifth day before the last day on which legislature may consider bills (in even-number years), legislature automatically reconvenes on first Wednesday following the second Monday in September for a maximum 10-calendar day session. *New Jersey*—legislature meets in special session (without call or petition) to act on bills returned by governor on 45th day after sine die adjournment of the regular session; if the second year expires before the 45th day, the day preceding the end of the legislative year. *Utah*—if 2/3 of the members of each house favor reconvening to consider vetoed bills, a maximum five-day session is set by the presiding officers. *Virginia*—legislature reconvenes on sixth Wednesday after adjournment for a maximum three-day session (may be extended to seven days upon vote of majority of members elected to each house). *Washington*—upon petition of 2/3 of the members of each house, legislature meets 45 days after adjournment for a maximum five-day session.

Key:

A—days after adjournment of legislature
P—days after presentation to governor

(a) Sundays excluded, unless otherwise indicated.
(b) Includes language in appropriations bill.
(c) Bill returned to house of origin with governor's objections.
(d) Governor can also reduce amounts in appropriations bills. In Hawaii, governor can reduce items in executive appropriations measures, but cannot reduce nor item veto amounts appropriated for the judicial or legislative branches.
(e) Different number of votes required for revenue and appropriations bills. Alaska—3/4 elected. Illinois—appropriations reductions, majority elected. Oklahoma—emergency bills, 3/4 vote. West Virginia—budget and supplemental appropriations, 2/3 elected.
(f) Sundays included.
(g) A bill presented to the governor that is not returned within 12 days (excluding Saturdays, Sundays, and holidays) becomes a law; provided that nay bill passed before Sept. 1 of the second calendar year of the biennium of the legislative session and in the possession of the governor on or after Sept. 1 that is not returned by the governor on or before Sept. 30 of that year becomes law. The legislature

Vetoes and Veto Override (continued)

may not present to the governor any bill after Nov. 15 of the second calendar year of the biennium of the session. If the legislature, by adjournment of a special session prevents the return of a bill with the veto message, the bill becomes law unless the governor vetoes within 12 days be depositing it and the veto message in the office of the secretary of state.

(h) Constitution withholds right to veto constitutional amendments.

(i) Bills vetoed after adjournment are returned to the legislature for reconsideration. Georgia: bills vetoed during last three days of session and not considered for overriding, and all bills vetoed after sine die adjournment may be considered at next session. Maine: returned within three days after the next meeting of the same legislature which enacted the bill or resolution. Maryland: reconsidered at the next meeting of the same General Assembly. Mississippi: returned within three days after the beginning of the next session. Missouri: bills returned on or after the 5th day before the last day to consider bills—legislature automatically reconvenes on the first Wednesday following the second Wednesday in September not to exceed 10 calendar days. South Carolina: within two days after the next meeting.

(j) Except Sundays and legal holidays. In Hawaii, except Saturdays, Sundays, holidays, and any days in which the legislature is in recess prior to its adjournment. In Oregon, except Saturdays and Sundays.

(k) The governor must notify the legislature 10 days before the 45th day of his intent to veto a measure on that day. The legislature may convene on the 45th day after adjournment to consider the vetoed measures. If the legislature fails to reconvene, the bill does not become law. If the legislature reconvenes, it may pass the measure over the governor's veto or it may amend the law to meet the governor's objections. If the law is amended, the governor must sign the bill within 10 days after it is presented to him in order for it to become law.

(l) Governor must sign or veto all bills presented to him. Any bill submitted to the governor for his approval during the last three days of a session must be deposited by him in the secretary of state's office within 30 days after adjournment with his approval or objections.

(m) No appropriation can be made in excess of the recommendations contained in the governor's budget except by a 3/5 vote. The excess is subject to veto by the governor.

(n) On the 45th day after the date of presentation, a bill becomes law unless the governor returns it with his objections, except that (1) if the legislature is in adjournment sine die on the 45th day, a special session is convened (without petition or call) for the sole purpose of acting upon bills returned by the governor; (2) any bill passed between the 45th day and 10th day preceding the end of the second legislative year must be returned by the governor by the day preceding the end of the second legislative year; (3) any bill passed or reenacted within 10 days preceding the expiration of the second legislative year becomes law if signed prior to the seventh day following such expiration, or the governor returns it to the house of origin and 2/3 elected members agree to pass the bill prior to such expiration.

(o) Governor has no approval or veto power.

(p) Must include majority of elected members

© 1994–95 The Council of State Governments. Reprinted with permission from *The Book of the States*.

164

2. Names of State Legislative Bodies

State	Both bodies	Upper house	Lower house
Alabama	Legislature	Senate	House of Representatives
Alaska	Legislature	Senate	House of Representatives
Arizona	Legislature	Senate	House of Representatives
Arkansas	General Assembly	Senate	House of Representatives
California	Legislature	Senate	Assembly
Colorado	General Assembly	Senate	House of Representatives
Connecticut	General Assembly	Senate	House of Representatives
Delaware	General Assembly	Senate	House of Representatives
Florida	Legislature	Senate	House of Representatives
Georgia	General Assembly	Senate	House of Representatives
Hawaii	Legislature	Senate	House of Representatives
Idaho	Legislature	Senate	House of Representatives
Illinois	General Assembly	Senate	House of Representatives
Indiana	General Assembly	Senate	House of Representatives
Iowa	General Assembly	Senate	House of Representatives
Kansas	Legislature	Senate	House of Representatives
Kentucky	General Assembly	Senate	House of Representatives
Louisiana	Legislature	Senate	House of Representatives
Maine	Legislature	Senate	House of Representatives
Maryland	General Assembly	Senate	House of Delegates
Massachusetts	General Court	Senate	House of Representatives
Michigan	Legislature	Senate	House of Representatives
Minnesota	Legislature	Senate	House of Representatives
Mississippi	Legislature	Senate	House of Representatives
Missouri	General Assembly	Senate	House of Representatives
Montana	Legislature	Senate	House of Representatives
Nebraska	Legislature	Senate (Unicameral)	
Nevada	Legislature	Senate	Assembly
New Hampshire	General Court	Senate	House of Representatives
New Jersey	Legislature	Senate	General Assembly
New Mexico	Legislature	Senate	House of Representatives
New York	Legislature	Senate	Assembly
North Carolina	General Assembly	Senate	House of Representatives
North Dakota	Legislative Assembly	Senate	House of Representatives
Ohio	General Assembly	Senate	House of Representatives
Oklahoma	Legislature	Senate	House of Representatives
Oregon	Legislative Assembly	Senate	House of Representatives
Pennsylvania	General Assembly	Senate	House of Representatives
Rhode Island	General Assembly	Senate	House of Representatives
South Carolina	General Assembly	Senate	House of Representatives
South Dakota	Legislature	Senate	House of Representatives
Tennessee	General Assembly	Senate	House of Representatives
Texas	Legislature	Senate	House of Representatives
Utah	Legislature	Senate	House of Representatives
Vermont	General Assembly	Senate	House of Representatives
Virginia	General Assembly	Senate	House of Delegates
Washington	Legislature	Senate	House of Representatives
West Virginia	Legislature	Senate	House of Delegates

Names of State Legislative Bodies *(continued)*

State	Both bodies	Upper house	Lower house
Wisconsin	Legislature	Senate	Assembly (a)
Wyoming	Legislature	Senate	House of Representatives

(a) Members of the lower house in Wisconsin go by the title Representative.
© 1994–95 The Council of State Governments. Reprinted with permission from *The Book of the States.*

3. State Legislators: Number and Terms

State	Senate		House		Senate and
	Total	Term	Total	Term	House Totals
All states	1,984		5,440		7,424
Alabama	35	4	105	4	140
Alaska	20	4	40	2	60
Arizona	30	2	60	2	90
Arkansas	35	4	100	2	135
California	40	4	80	2	120
Colorado	35	4	65	2	100
Connecticut	36	2	151	2	187
Delaware	21	4	41	2	62
Florida	40	4	120	2	160
Georgia	56	2	180	2	236
Hawaii	25	4	51	2	76
Idaho	35 (a)	2	70 (a)	2	105
Illinois	59	4 (b)	118	2	177
Indiana	50	4	100	2	150
Iowa	50	4	100	2	150
Kansas	40	4	125	2	165
Kentucky	38	4	100	2	138
Louisiana	39	4	105	4	144
Maine	35	2	151	2	186
Maryland	47	4	141	4	188
Massachusetts	40	2	160	2	200
Michigan	38	4	110	2	148
Minnesota	67	4	134	2	201
Mississippi	52	4	122	4	174
Missouri	34	4	163	2	197
Montana	50	4 (c)	100	2	150
Nebraska	49	4			49
Nevada	21	4	42	2	63
New Hampshire	24	2	400	2	424
New Jersey	40	4 (d)	80	2	120
New Mexico	42	4	70	2	112
New York	61	2	150	2	211
North Carolina	50	2	120	2	170
North Dakota	49 (e)	4	98 (e)	2	147
Ohio	33	4	99	2	132
Oklahoma	48	4	101	2	149
Oregon	30	4	60	2	90
Pennsylvania	50	4	203	2	253
Rhode Island	50	2	100	2	150
South Carolina	46	4	124	2	170
South Dakota	35	4	70	2	105
Tennessee	33	4	99	2	132
Texas	31	4	150	2	181
Utah	29	4	75	2	104
Vermont	30	2	150	2	180

State Legislators: Number and Terms (*continued*)

State	Senate Total	Senate Term	House Total	House Term	Senate and House Totals
Virginia	40	4	100	2	140
Washington	49	4	98	2	147
West Virginia	34	4	100	2	134
Wisconsin	33	4	99	2	132
Wyoming	30	4	60 (f)	2	90

(a) As a result of redistricting, membership of the legislature decreased: Senate from 42 to 35 members, House from 84 to 70 members.

(b) The entire Senate is up for election every 10 years, beginning in 1972. Senate districts are divided into three groups. One group elects senators for terms of 4 years, 4 years and 2 years, the second group for terms of 4 years, 2 years and 4 years, the third group for terms of 2 years, 4 years, and 4 years.

(c) After each decennial reapportionment, lots are drawn for half of the senators to serve an initial 2-year term. Subsequent elections are for 4-year terms.

(d) Senate terms beginning in January of second year following the U.S. decennial census are for 2 years only.

(e) As a result of redistricting, membership of the legislature decreased: Senate from 53 to 49, House from 106 to 98 members.

(f) As a result of redistricting, membership of the House decreased from 64 to 60 members.

4. Election Qualifications for State Legislators

State	House				Senate			
	Minimum age	U.S. citizen (years)	State resident (years)	District resident (years)	Minimum age	U.S. Citizen (years)	State resident (years)	District resident (years)
Alabama	21	...	3 (a)	1	25	...	3 (a)	1
Alaska	21	...	3	1	25	...	3	1
Arizona	25	*	3	1	25	*	3	1
Arkansas	21	*	2	1	25	*	2	1
California	18	3	3	1	18	3	3	1
Colorado	25	*	...	1	25	*	...	1
Connecticut	18	...	...	*	18	...	...	*
Delaware	24	...	3 (a)	1	27	...	3 (a)	1
Florida	21	...	2	*	21	...	2	*
Georgia	21	*	2 (a)	1	25	*	2 (a)	1
Hawaii	18	...	3	(b)	18	...	3	(b)
Idaho	18	*	...	1	18	*	...	1
Illinois	21	*	...	2 (c)	21	*	...	2 (c)
Indiana	21	*	2	1	25	*	2	1
Iowa	21	*	1	60 days	25	*	1	60 days
Kansas	18	...	...	*	18	...	...	*
Kentucky	24	...	2 (a)	1	30	...	6 (a)	1
Louisiana	18	...	2	1	18	...	2	1
Maine	21	5	1	3 mo.	25	5	1	3 mo.
Maryland	21	...	1 (a)	6 mo.(d)	25	...	1 (a)	6 mo.(d)
Massachusetts	18	...	...	1	18	*	5	*
Michigan	21	*	...	(b)	21	...	...	(b)
Minnesota	21	...	1	6 mo.	21	...	1	6 mo.
Mississippi	21	...	4 (a)	2	25	...	...	2
Missouri	24	...	...	1 (e)	30	...	...	1 (e)
Montana	18	...	1	6 mo.(f)	18	...	1	6 mo.(f)

Election Qualifications for State Legislators (*continued*)

	House				Senate			
	Minimum age	U.S. citizen (years)	State resident (years)	District resident (years)	Minimum age	U.S. Citizen (years)	State resident (years)	District resident (years)
Nebraska	U	U	U	U	21	...	...	1
Nevada	21	...	1 (a)	1	21	...	1 (a)	1
New Hampshire	18	...	2	*	30	...	7	*
New Jersey	21	...	2 (a)	1	30	...	4 (a)	1
New Mexico	21	...	...	*	25	...	...	*
New York	18	*	5	1 (g)	18	*	5	1 (g)
North Carolina	(h)	*	1	1	25	*	2 (a)	1
North Dakota	18	...	1	(b)	18	...	1	(b)
Ohio	18	...	...	1	18	...	...	1
Oklahoma	21	...	...	(b)	25	...	...	(b)
Oregon	21	*	...	1	21	*	4 (a)	1
Pennsylvania	21	...	4 (a)	1	25	...	4 (a)	1
Rhode Island	18	...	...	...	18	...	...	...
South Carolina	21	...	...	(b)	25	...	...	(b)
South Dakota	25	*	2	(b)	25	*	2	(b)
Tennessee	21	*	3 (a)	1 (b)	30	*	3	1 (b)
Texas	21	*	2	1	26	*	5	1
Utah	25	*	3	6 mo.(b)	25	*	3	6 mo.(b)
Vermont	18	...	2	1	18	...	2	1
Virginia	21	*	1	*	21	*	1	*
Washington	18	*	...	(b)	18	*	...	(b)
West Virginia	18	...	5(a)	1	25	...	5 (a)	1
Wisconsin	18	...	1	(b)	18	...	1	(b)
Wyoming	21	*	(a)	1	25	*	(a)	1

Election Qualifications for State Legislators (*continued*)

Key:
U Unicameral legislature; members are called senators.
* Formal provision; number of years not specified.
... No formal provision.

(a) State citizenship requirement.

(b) Must be a qualified voter of the district; number of years not specified.

(c) Following redistricting, a candidate may be elected from any district that contains a part of the district in which he resided at the time of redistricting, and reelected if a resident of the new district he represents for 18 months prior to reelection.

(d) If the district was established for less than six months, residency is length of establishment of district.

(e) Only if the district has been in existence for one year; if not, then legislator must have been a one year resident of the district(s) from which the new district was created.

(f) Shall be a resident of the county if it contains one or more districts or of the district if it contains all or parts of more than one county.

(g) After redistricting, must have been a resident of the county in which the district is contained for one year immediately preceding election.

(h) A conflict exists between two articles of the constitution, one specifying age for House members (i.e., "qualified voter of the state") and the other related to general eligibility for elective office (i.e., "every qualified voter ... who is 21 years of age ... shall be eligible for election").

© 1994–95 The Council of State Governments. Reprinted with permission from *The Book of the States*

5. Sources of Information about Your State Legislature

State	Senate General Information	Senate Copies of bills, etc.	Senate Bill status update	House General information	House Copies of bills, etc.	House Bill status update
Alabama	(205) 242-7800	(205) 242-7826	(205) 242-7826	(205) 242-7600	(205) 242-7637	(205) 242-7627
Alaska	(907) 465-4648	(907) 465-3737 (907) 465-4648*	(907) 465-4648	(907) 465-4648	(907) 465-3737 (907) 465-4648*	(907) 465-4648
Arizona	(602) 542-3559	(602) 542-4379 (602) 542-4231*	(602) 542-3559	(602) 542-4221	(602) 542-4379 (602) 542-3032*	(602) 542-4221
Arkansas	(501) 682-5954	(501) 682-2902 (501) 682-6107*	(501) 682-2902 (501) 682-6107*	(501) 682-7771	(501) 682-7771	(501) 682-7771
California	(916) 445-4251	(916) 445-2323	(916) 445-4251	(916) 445-3614	(916) 445-2323	(916) 445-3614
Colorado	(303) 866-3521	(303) 866-2340 (303) 866-2316*	(303) 866-3055 (303) 866-3521	(303) 866-3521	(303) 866-2340 (303) 866-2904*	(303) 866-3055 (303) 866-3521*
Connecticut	(203) 566-4544	(203) 240-0333	(203) 566-4601 (203) 566-3900*	(203) 566-4544	(203) 240-0333	(203) 566-4601 (203) 566-3900*
Delaware	(302) 739-4114	(302) 739-4114	(302) 739-4114	(302) 739-4114	(302) 739-4114	(302) 739-4114
Florida	(904) 488-4371	(904)487-5285	(904) 488-4371	(904) 488-4371	(904)487-7475	(904) 488-4371
Georgia	(404) 656-5040	(404) 656-5040	(404) 656-5040	(404) 656-5015	(404) 656-5015	(404) 656-5015
Hawaii	(808) 586-6720	(808) 586-6755	(808) 587-0700	(808) 586-6400	(808) 685-6400	(808) 587-0700
Idaho	(208) 334-2475	(208) 334-3012 (208) 334-3175*	(208) 334-3175	(208) 334-2475	(208) 334-3012 (208) 334-3175*	(208) 334-3175
Illinois	(217) 782-6851	(217) 782-9778	(217) 782-3944	(217) 782-6851	(217) 782-5799	(217) 782-3944
Indiana	(317) 232-9856	(317) 232-9856	(317) 232-9856	(317) 232-9856	(317) 232-9856	(317) 232-9856
Iowa	(515) 281-5129	(515) 281-5129	(515) 281-5129	(515) 281-5129	(515) 281-5129	(515) 281-5129
Kansas	(913) 296-2391	(913) 296-4096 (913) 296-2391*	(913) 296-3296	(913) 296-2391	(913) 296-4096 (913) 296-2391*	(913) 296-3296
Kentucky	(502)564-8100	(502) 564-8100, ext. 323	(502) 564-2500 (502) 564-8100*	(502)564-8100	(502) 564-8100, ext. 323	(502) 564-2500 (502) 564-8100*
Louisiana	(504) 342-2431	(504) 342-2192 (504) 342-2365*	(800) 256-3793	(504) 342-2431	(504) 342-2192 (504) 342-6458*	(800) 256-3793 (504) 342-2456*
Maine	(207) 287-1540	(207) 287-1500	(207) 287-1692	(207) 287-1400	(207) 287-1408	(207) 287-1692
Maryland	(410) 841-3810	(410) 841-3810	(410) 841-3810	(410) 841-3810	(410) 841-3810	(410) 841-3810
Massachusetts	(617) 722-1276	(617) 722-2860	(617) 722-2860	(617) 722-2356	(617) 722-2860	(617) 722-2860
Michigan	(517) 373-2400	(517) 373-0169	(517) 373-0169	(517) 373-0135	(517) 373-0169	(517) 373-0169
Minnesota	(612) 296-0504	(612) 296-2343	(612) 296-6646	(612) 296-2146	(612) 296-2314	(612) 296-6646
Mississippi	(601) 359-3202	(601) 359-3719 (601) 359-3229*	(601) 359-3719 (601) 359-3229*	(601) 359-3360	(601) 359-3719 (601) 359-3358*	(601) 359-3719 (601) 359-3358*

Sources of Information about Your State Legislature (continued)

State	Senate			House		
	General Information	Copies of bills, etc.	Bill status update	General information	Copies of bills, etc.	Bill status update
Missouri	(314) 751-4633	(314) 751-2966	(314) 751-4633	(314) 751-4633	(314) 751-3968	(314) 751-4633
Montana	(406) 444-3064	(406) 444-0627 (406) 444-3064*	(406) 444-4853	(406) 444-3064	(406) 444-0627 (406) 444-3064*	(406) 444-4853
Nebraska	(402) 471-2271	(402) 471-2609 (402) 471-2271*	(402) 471-2271	U	U	U
Nevada	(702) 687-6800 (702) 687-6835*	(702) 687-3560	(702) 687-5545 (702) 687-5160*	(702) 687-6800	(702) 687-3560 (702) 687-6835*	(702) 687-5545 (702) 687-5160*
New Hampshire	(603) 271-2239	(603) 271-2239	(603) 271-2239	(603) 271-2239	(603) 271-2239	(603) 271-2239
New Jersey	(609) 292-4840	(609) 292-6395	(609) 292-4840	(609) 292-4840	(609) 292-6395	(609) 292-4840
New Mexico	(505) 986-4714	(505) 827-4011 (505) 986-4600*	(505) 986-4600	(505) 986-4751	(505) 827-4011 (505) 986-4600*	(505) 986-4600
New York	(518) 455-2051	(518) 455-2311	(518) 455-7545	(518) 455-4218	(518) 455-5165	(518) 455-7545
North Carolina	(919) 733-7044	(919) 733-5648	(919) 733-7779	(919) 733-7044	(919) 733-5648	(919) 733-7779
North Dakota	(701) 328-2916	(701) 328-3248	(701) 328-3373 (701) 328-2916, ask for library	(701) 328-2916	(701) 328-3248	(701) 328-3373 (701) 328-2916, ask for library
Ohio	(614) 466-8842	(614) 466-7168	(614) 466-8842	(614) 466-8842	(614) 466-8207	(614) 466-8842
Oklahoma	(405) 521-2502, ext. 280	(405) 521-5515	(405) 521-5642	(405) 521-2502, ext. 280	(405) 521-5515	(405) 521-2733
Oregon	(503) 378-8179	(503) 986-1180	(503) 986-1180	(503) 378-8179	(503) 986-1180	(503) 986-1180
Pennsylvania	(717) 787-6732	(717) 787-6732	(717) 787-2342	(717) 787-5320	(717) 787-5320	(717) 787-2342
Rhode Island	(401) 277-2473	(401) 277-2473	(401) 751-8833	(401) 277-2473	(401) 277-2473	(401) 751-8833
South Carolina	(803) 734-2311	(803) 734-2060	(803) 734-2060	(803) 734-2402	(803) 734-2060	(803) 734-2060
South Dakota	(605) 773-3251	(605) 773-3835 (605) 773-3251*	(605) 773-4498	(605) 773-3251	(605) 773-3835 (605) 773-3251*	(605) 773-4498
Tennessee	(615) 741-3511	(615) 741-0496 (615) 741-3511*	(615) 741-0927	(615) 741-3511	(615) 741-0496 (615) 741-3511*	(615) 741-0927
Texas	(512) 463-1252	(512) 463-1144	(512) 463-1251	(512) 463-1252	(512) 463-1144	(512) 463-1251
Utah	(801) 538-1032	(801) 538-1035	(801) 538-1035	(801) 538-1032	(801) 538-1029	(801) 538-1029
Vermont	(802) 828-2231	(802) 828-2231	(802) 828-2231	(802) 828-2231	(802) 828-2231	(802) 828-2231
Virginia	(804) 786-6530	(804) 786-6984	(804) 786-6530	(804) 786-6530	(804) 786-6984	(804) 786-6530
Washington	(206) 786-7550	(206) 786-7573	(206)786-7573	(206) 786-7550	(206) 786-7573	(206)786-7573
West Virginia	(304) 347-4800	(304) 357-7947 (304) 347-4831*	(304) 347-4831	(304) 347-4800	(304) 357-3244 (304) 347-4831*	(304) 347-4831

Sources of Information about Your State Legislature (*continued*)

State	Senate			House		
	General Information	Copies of bills, etc.	Bill status update	General information	Copies of bills, etc.	Bill status update
Wisconsin	(608) 266-0341	(608) 266-2400	(608) 266-9960	(608) 266-0341	(608) 266-2400	(608) 266-9960
Wyoming	(307) 777-7881	(307) 777-7648	(307) 777-6185	(307) 777-7881	(307) 777-7648	(307) 777-7765
		(307) 777-7881*	(307) 777-7881*		(307) 777-7881*	(307) 777-7881*

Key:
U   Unicameral
*   Between session phone number

6. Average Size of Legislative Districts*

State	Senates		Houses	
	Members	District Population	Members	District Population
Alabama	35	116,086	105	38,695
Alaska	20	27,600	40	13,800
Arizona	30	122,600	60	61,300
Arkansas	35	67,486	100	23,620
California	40	745,975	80	372,988
Colorado	35	94,514	65	50,892
Connecticut	36	91,556	151	21,828
Delaware	21	31,857	41	16,317
Florida	40	325,075	120	108,358
Georgia	56	116,214	180	36,156
Hawaii	25	44,600	51	21,863
Idaho	35	28,914	70	14,457
Illinois	59	194,356	118	97,178
Indiana	50	111,280	100	55,640
Iowa	50	55,740	100	27,870
Kansas	40	62,150	125	19,888
Kentucky	38	97,342	100	36,990
Louisiana	39	108,667	105	40,362
Maine	35	35,229	151	8,166
Maryland	47	102,106	141	34,035
Massachusetts	40	150,725	160	37,681
Michigan	38	245,500	110	84,809
Minnesota	67	65,478	134	32,739
Mississippi	52	49,731	122	21,197
Missouri	34	151,118	163	31,521
Montana	50	16,080	100	8,040
Nebraska	49	32,347	NA	
Nevada	21	57,429	42	28,714
New Hampshire	24	46,417	400	2,785
New Jersey	40	193,725	80	96,863
New Mexico	42	36,238	70	21,743
New York	61	295,820	150	120,300
North Carolina	50	133,160	120	55,483
North Dakota	49	13,082	98	6,541
Ohio	33	3a29,909	99	109,970
Oklahoma	48	65,792	101	31,267
Oregon	30	95,133	60	47,567
Pennsylvania	50	238,500	203	58,744
Rhode Island	50	20,120	100	10,060
South Carolina	46	76,217	124	28,274
South Dakota	35	20,000	70	10,000
Tennessee	33	148,394	99	49,465
Texas	31	550,323	150	113,733
Utah	29	59,586	75	23,040
Vermont	30	18,833	150	3,767
Virginia	40	155,425	100	62,170
Washington	49	99,755	98	49,878
West Virginia	34	53,000	100	18,020
Wisconsin	33	148,697	99	49,566
Wyoming	30	15,200	60	7,600
Congress	100	NA	435	572,476

* Based on 1990 population statistics

7. Tips for Testifying before a Legislative Committee*

You have the right...

- You have the right, as do all citizens, to testify before the North Dakota Legislative Assembly on any bill or resolution.
- North Dakota has one of the most *open* legislatures in the nation. Every bill must have a public hearing before a legislative committee, must be publicly voted upon by the committee, and then must come before the full House or Senate for still another public vote.
- Your opportunity to testify on a bill comes at the committee hearing.
- Legislative committees meet in rooms scattered around the House and Senate chambers in the State Capitol. **You can come into a committee meeting at any time, even if the door is closed or a hearing is in progress.**
- Lists of the legislative committees, committee members, and the days and places committees meet are available at the Legislative Information Kiosk in the hall between Senate and House chambers.
- You can find out which committee will be hearing the bill in which you are interested by calling the toll-free number and asking for information or inquiring in person at the Legislative Information Kiosk. Also, most of the state's daily newspapers carry listings of all the bills that are introduced and of scheduled committee hearings.
- In addition to checking with the Legislative Information Kiosk, you can find out what bills are being heard by what committees by reviewing the TV monitors on the Kiosk and in the hall of the ground floor of the Capitol. All committee hearings are listed on these monitors weekly.
- You can get copies of bills from the Bill and Journal Room. However, if the bill has been amended, the printed bill may not include the amendments.

---

* From the North Dakota Legislative Council

Hearings before North Dakota Legislative Committees Are Generally Informal and Few Rules Need Be Observed!

Before the Hearing You Should...

- Find out when and where your bill will be heard. Be on time for the hearing. Usually, once a hearing is closed on a particular bill, no further testimony will be heard.
- Plan your testimony. It is not necessary, but it is helpful, to have written copies of your comments available.
- See if other persons will be testifying on your bill. If so, try to coordinate your testimony prior to the hearing to avoid duplication.
- Contact the Secretary of State's office if you are going to testify on behalf of anyone but yourself, to see if you must register as a lobbyist.

At the Hearing You Should...

- Be present at the start of the hearing. All persons present usually get a chance to speak, but sometimes, because of large turnouts, it is not possible to give everyone a chance to speak. If you do not get a chance to testify, your presence may be acknowledged and you might be asked if you favor or oppose the bill. And, you can always submit written testimony.
- Sign the witness sheet at the lectern or at the end of the table where you'll testify. Give your name, the bill number and if you favor or oppose it.
- Wait your turn. The chair announces the beginning of the hearing on a particular bill. The clerk will read the bill. The first speaker is usually the bill's sponsor. The chair then asks for testimony from proponents and opponents.
- Plan on following the custom (although it is not absolutely necessary) of beginning your remarks by addressing the chair and committee members giving your name and address, and why you are there. For example: "Mr. or Madam Chair, and members of the committee, my name is John Q. Public from Edwinton. I'm in favor of this bill because, etc."

- Be brief. Do not repeat what others have said. The hearings are informal, so be conversational. Avoid being too technical.
- Do not be nervous, or worried about doing something wrong. There are no "rights and wrongs" about testifying. Legislators are just your friends and neighbors who want to hear what you have to say.
- Expect some questions and comments from committee members. These questions are not designed to embarrass you, but merely to provide additional information.
- Avoid any clapping, cheering, booing, or other demonstrations.

After the Hearing...

- Some committees vote right after a hearing. Others wait until the end of the meeting. And some postpone until another meeting.
- Remember, all committee action, including a vote, is public, so you can stay to listen to the committee debate and its vote, even though the public comment portion of the hearing is over.
- One or two days later you can check with the committee clerk, your legislator, or the Legislative Information Kiosk to find out how the committee voted on your bill.

Remember, you have a right to testify on any bill before a legislative committee. Legislators want to hear what you have to say.

MATERIALS
AVAILABLE FROM
STATE
LEGISLATURES

• • • • • • • • •

Thuis is an informal listing of a variety of materials from several states. There has been no attempt to rank them in any order, and no attempt to suggest which may be more useful than others. Every state legislature makes information available to the public and to schools about the specifics of the legislative process in that state. The materials available from the states are informative and uniformly well done.

The following list is not intended to be comprehensive. It is a representative sample of the type of educational materials that are available from state legislatures everywhere.

Alabama   *The Legislative Process: A Handbook for Alabama Legislators.* Alabama Law Institute, Tuscaloosa.
The Legislative Process: A Teacher's Guide. Alabama Law Institute, Tuscaloosa.
These materials are very well done, and they are updated every four years. The Law Institute has also produced an excellent 20-minute video on the legislative process: "Be it Enacted."

California *California's Legislature.* A comprehensive book by the Chief Clerk of the Assembly. Includes information on the California constitution, elections, and the executive and judicial branches.

Iowa   The Legislative Information Office produces an information packet that covers every aspect of the legislature in a brief, easy to read format. It includes, among other things, briefs on the differences between the Iowa and U.S. legislatures, recent ethics legislation, how to lobby, the legislative process, a session timetable, a glossary, and a state capitol tour quiz.

Kentucky *A Look at the Kentucky General Assembly.* Legislative Research Commission. A brief booklet that covers the basics. A number of states publish information in the same format.

Maryland *Your Voice in Annapolis: Maryland General Assembly.* Most of this publication is devoted to identifying the current members. There are a few pages, very basic, on the process.

Legislative Lingo. A glossary. This is something that many states include in their public information materials.

Minnesota *Inside the Senate,* 1990 Edition. A good publication. Question and answer format (111 questions).

How Six Bills Became Law. House Public Information Office, 1990. A little booklet—32 pages—that is exceptionally well done.

People and the Process: A Legislative Study Guide. House Public Information Office, 1991. Excellent for use in the public schools. Includes extensive indices that cover all aspects of the legislature and much of state government.

Montana *The Montana Legislative Process: Instruction for Montana's Youth.*

Nebraska *A Student Guide to the Nebraska Legislature.* It is different from most. Cartoon style, which many states use, but very well done— and in color.

Nevada *The Nevada Legislative Manual* has a chapter entitled, "The Legislature in Action: A Bill Becomes a Law."

Utah *State and Local Government in Utah.* Utah Foundation, 1992. A private sector publication, comprehensive in its coverage of state government.

Wisconsin *The Legislative Process in Wisconsin.* A reprint from Wisconsin's Blue Book, the 1993–94 edition. It is very well done.

GLOSSARY OF LEGISLATIVE LANGUAGE

· · · · · · · · ·

Legislators speak a language all their own, using terms that have a special meaning in the legislative process. The following definitions of some of that language are excerpts from: *Glossary of Legislative and Computer Terms*, a publication of the American Society of Legislative Clerks & Secretaries.

Adhere. A parliamentary procedure in which, in response to conflicting action by the other house, one house of the legislature votes to stand by its previous action. The result usually would be a request for a conference committee to resolve the differences.

Adjournment. Termination of a session for that day, with the hour and day of the next meeting being set prior to adjournment.

Adjournment sine die. Final termination of a regular or special legislative session.

Adoption. Approval or acceptance. Usually applied to amendments, committee reports, or resolutions.

Agenda. Schedule of business proposed for each legislative day.

Amend. To alter formally by modification, deletion, or addition.

Amendment. A change proposed or made to a bill or motion. Amendments may be offered by committees or individual legislators.

Amendment, Constitutional. Resolution passed by both houses which affects the Constitution. Requires approval by voters at a general election.

Amendment, floor. An amendment offered to a legislative document, or offered to modify another amendment, presented by a legislator while the document is on the floor of that legislator's house.

Appropriation. State money allocated by the legislature for use by departments of state government.

Assembly. That house of the legislature made up of a certain number of members, elected from districts apportioned on the basis of population.

Bicameral. A legislature containing two houses.

Biennium. Two-year term of legislative activity.

Bill. Draft of a proposed law presented to the legislature for consideration.

Bill history. Record of all the action on any given proposal. The term is also applied to action on resolutions and joint resolutions.

Bill index. List of legislative bills by subject matter or number.

Bill, laid over. A parliamentary procedure that allows a bill to which there is a proposed amendment to lie over one day under the rules. It may also be accomplished by motion.

Bill, prefiled. Bills prepared and filed prior to the opening of a regular session.

Bloc. A group of legislators who have certain interests in common and who may vote together on matters affecting that interest.

Budget. Suggested allocation of money for state programs and departments.

Budget, executive. Suggested allocation of state money presented by the governor for consideration by the legislature.

By request. The phrase "by request" may be added after the name of the member introducing a bill, indicating that it has been introduced at the request of a constituent, a government agency, or an organization.

Calendar. Printed list of proposals, arranged according to the order of business, which is scheduled for consideration on a legislative day. In some states, includes the history of legislative measures by their number and chronological listing of action taken. Also shows dates of hearings and other statistical material.

Calendar, consent. Bills placed on this calendar are non-controversial measures. A bill placed on the consent calendar is not subject to amendment, except for committee amendments.

Calendar, session. Numerical list of bills and resolutions considered during a legislative session, giving actions on each.

Call of the Senate or House. Procedure used to compel attendance of members and to compel those in attendance to remain in the chamber.

Call to order. The action of the presiding officer that brings the legislature officially into session. It may also be used to call a disorderly member to order.

Carry-over legislation. Legislation held over from one annual session of the legislature to the next, during the two-year period that constitutes a General Assembly. For example, a state legislature's 60th General Assembly would convene in 1996 and 1997, which would indicate that the legislature had been in existence for 120 years.

Caucus. An informal meeting of a group of legislative members, sometimes called on the basis of party affiliation.

Chair. Presiding officer.

Chamber. Official hall for the meeting of a legislative body.

Code. A compilation of laws on a given subject; the official publication of the statutes.

Commit. Action to send a measure to a committee, even though it had been previously reported.

Committee. A body of elected members delegated by a legislative body to consider and make recommendations on bills, resolutions, and other related matters often restricted to certain subject areas.

Committee, ad hoc. A committee appointed for some special purpose. The committee automatically dissolves upon the completion of its specified task.

Committee amendment. An amendment which is attached to a bill by a committee and made a part of the committee's report.

Committee chair. A member appointed to function as the parliamentary head of a standing or special committee to consider matters assigned to the committee.

Committee, conference. A group of legislators appointed by the Senate and House to resolve differences between the two chambers on a bill. There are two types of Conference committees: free and limited. Free Conference committees are allowed to make any changes necessary to reach agreement on a bill that has been passed by both legislative chambers, but in different versions. Limited Conference committees are limited to reaching agreement only on the differences between the versions of a bill that has been passed by both legislative chambers.

Committee, interim. A committee created to study legislative proposals or other legislative matters during the time the legislature is not in session and to make recommendations to the next regular session of the legislature.

Committee, joint. Committee composed of members of both houses.

Committee report. An official release from a committee on a bill or resolution with a specific recommendation or without recommendation.

Committee, select. Committee appointed to consider and make recommendations for specific proposals. Also a committee formed to work between sessions on a particular proposal.

Committee, standing. A committee appointed with a continuing responsibility in a general field of legislative activity.

Committee substitute. A bill offered by a committee in lieu of a bill it has considered. The committee substitute is an amendment to the original bill.

Committee of the Whole. A parliamentary process in which all the members of a chamber meet as a committee, rather than as a legislative body, to consider bills. The chair for a Committee of the Whole is appointed by the chamber's presiding officer.

Concurrence. Action by which one house agrees to a proposal or action which the other house has approved. A proposal may be amended, adopted, and then returned to the other house for concurrence.

Constituent. A citizen residing within the district of a legislator.

Constitution. A written document embodying the fundamental principles of the state that guarantees powers and duties of the government and guarantees certain rights to the people.

Constitutional majority. One more than half of the members of a deliberative body.

Convene. The gathering of the legislature at the beginning of the legislative session.

Co-sponsor. One of two or more legislators proposing any bill or resolution.

Debate. Discussion of a matter according to parliamentary rules.

Desk. The desk at the front of the chamber where much of the clerical work of a legislative body is conducted. Also, a generic term for the staff and offices of the secretary of the Senate and the clerk of the Assembly or House.

Desk is clear. Statement by presiding officer, prior to motion to adjourn, meaning there is no further business to be conducted.

Died in committee. Measure defeated or not acted on in committee.

District. That division of the state represented by a legislator, distinguished numerically or by geographical boundaries.

Division. A method of voting: a request that members stand or raise hands to be counted when the outcome of a voice vote is unclear or in dispute.

Do pass. The affirmative recommendation made by a committee in sending a bill to the floor for action. "Do pass as amended" indicates that the committee recommends certain changes in the bill.

Effective date. A law becomes binding, either upon a date specified in the law itself or, in the absence of such a date, a certain number of days after final adjournment.

Enactment. Process by which a measure becomes a law.

Enacting clause. That clause of a bill which formally expresses the legislative sanction. It varies in different states but usually begins "Be it Enacted...."

Engrossed/perfected bill. An official copy of a bill or resolution as passed by one house, incorporating all changes and amendments.

Enrolled bill. The final copy of a bill passed by both houses of the legislature.

Executive order. Rule or decision of the governor.

Ex officio. The holding of a particular office by reason of holding another. For example, the Speaker of the House is by virtue of that office an ex officio member of all standing House committees.

File. Daily printed program or agenda of business before either chamber. A term used in some states in lieu of "bill."

First reading. To read the first of three times the bill or title for consideration. In most states the first reading is done at the time of introduction.

Filibuster. The extremely prolonged discussion of a bill in order to delay legislative action.

Floor. That portion of the assembly chamber reserved for members and officers of the assembly and other persons granted the privilege of the floor.

General file. Third reading file of bills and resolutions due for consideration by the members. Usually the final reading before a vote is taken on passage of the bill.

General orders. An order of legislative business in which the Committee of the Whole considers certain bills and related matters. Generally a more informal meeting allowing unlimited debate. Votes are usually not recorded.

Gerrymandering. Drawing legislative district boundary lines to obtain partisan or factional advantages.

Governor's proclamation. A means by which the governor may call an extra or special session of the legislature.

Germane. Relevant amendments or substitutes are referred to as germane.

Hearing. Scheduled public discussion and appearance on a proposal in committee.

Hopper. The presentation of a bill for formal introduction and first reading, or a figurative depository for bills filed for introduction.

House. A legislative body, more commonly known as the House of Representatives.

Impeachment. Procedure to remove from office public officials accused of misconduct.

Indefinite postponement. A parliamentary procedure maneuver to kill a bill.

Initiative. Citizen action to bypass the legislature which places proposed statutes and, in some states, constitutional amendments, on the ballot.

Insert. Add language to a bill or resolution.

Interim. The interval between regular sessions.

Introduction. The formal presentation of a proposal or bill after it has been processed or drafted.

Joint resolution/constitutional resolution. Proposal for a change in the state constitution which, if passed, goes to the voters for their approval. The resolution does not go to the governor and does not require his approval.

Joint rules. Adopted by both houses acting jointly at the beginning of the first regular session. These rules govern the procedures to be followed in all areas of joint legislative activity.

Joint session. Both houses meet together in one chamber.

Journal. An official chronological record of the proceedings and action taken of the respective houses.

Laid over. A postponement of consideration. Sometimes rules provide that a bill be laid over to allow time for printing of amendments.

Lay on the table. Postponement of the matter before the house, which may later be brought up for consideration by a motion to "take from the table."

Legislative council. Statutory nonpartisan legislative agency that provides bill drafting, impartial research, and information and technical services.

Legislative intent. Purpose for which a measure was passed.

Line item. Numeric line in an appropriation bill.

Line item veto. An action taken by the governor to prevent enactment of an item in an appropriation bill.

Majority caucus. The group numbering more than one-half of the membership of a legislative body.

Majority leader. A member of the majority party designated to be leader.

Majority, minority districts. Legislative districts whose boundaries are drawn to include a majority of a minority group living in the area.

Majority party. The political party having the greater number of members in the legislature or either house.

Majority whip. A member of the House or Senate designated to perform certain functions, such as determining how members of the majority party may vote on a bill.

Measure. Bill, resolution, or memorial.

Memorial. The method by which the legislature expresses its opinion to Congress and other governments or governmental agencies.

Minority leader. A member of the minority party designated to be leader.

Minority party. Party numbering the fewest members in the legislature or either house.

Minority report. A report that reflects the thinking of the members not favoring the majority position on an action.

Minority whip. A member of the minority party designated to perform functions related to the minority party's activities.

Motion. Formal proposal offered by a member of a deliberative assembly.

Order of business. The defined routine of procedure in the legislative body each day.

Out of order. Not being conducted under proper parliamentary rules and procedures.

Pair or pairing. An arrangement by two members of a house by which they agree to be recorded on opposite sides of a question when they expect to be absent the time that the vote is taken.

Point of order. Calling attention to a breach of order or rules.

Postpone indefinitely. A means of disposing of an issue and not setting a date to consider it again.

Postpone to a day certain. To defer consideration to a definite later time or day.

Prefiled bill. A bill filed with the clerk of the House or secretary of the Senate prior to the official convening of a session of the legislature.

President. Title of the person presiding over the Senate.

President Pro Tempore. The person elected by the Senate to have the same powers as the president in the latter's absence.

Presiding officer. The person designated to preside at a legislative session.

Previous question. A motion to close debate and bring the pending question to an immediate vote.

Quorum. The required number of members present to transact business.

Quorum call. A method used to establish the presence of a majority in order to transact business, often heard just before the vote on a controversial measure, putting legislators on notice that a significant vote is about to be taken.

Ratify. To approve.

Reading. Presentation of a bill before either house by reading the bill number or title. Most state constitutions require that bills receive three readings on three different days.

Reapportionment. Redrawing legislative district boundaries to produce equality of representation.

Recall. A procedure that allows citizens to remove an elected official before the end of the official's term of office.

Recall a bill. A motion which enables either house to recall a bill previously passed. In Texas a concurrent resolution must be passed in each house to accomplish this.

Recede. Withdraw from an amendment or position on a matter.

Recess. Intermission in a daily session or from one day to the next.

Recommit. To send back to committee.

Record. By custom, members often request that the "record" show or that they be "recorded" in a certain way. These requests, if approved, are entered in the journal.

Referendum. A method by which a measure adopted by the legislature must be submitted to popular vote to be approved or rejected.

Referral. The sending or referring of a bill to committee.

Re-refer. The reassignment of a bill or resolution to a committee.

Repeal. A method by which legislative action is revoked.

Report. To approve by committee.

Rescind. Annulment of a previous action.

Resolution, concurrent. A document expressing sentiment or intent of the legislature, governing the business of the legislature.

Resolution, joint. A means of amending the state constitution or to ratify an amendment to the U.S. constitution.

Resolution, Senate or House. Same as a concurrent resolution except that it is the expression of one house.

Revised code. Updated statutory laws of the state.

Rise and report progress. Used by Committee of the Whole to report a bill under consideration and send it on to third reading.

Roll call. The vote on an issue, either by an electrical tabulating machine or by voice vote. Names of members are called in alphabetical order and their vote is recorded.

Rules. Methods of procedure.

Ruling of the chair. A decision by the presiding officer concerning a question of order or procedure.

Second reading. The second reading of a bill. In some states the bill is referred to committee at second reading. In others, if the measure is approved, it moves to third reading, and still in others, it is passed to be engrossed.

Section. A portion of the state statutes, or codes, cited in each bill which proposes to amend, create, or replace a section of the statutes.

Session. Period during which the legislature meets. A regular session denotes the annual session at which all classes of legislation may be considered. Extraordinary or special sessions are limited to specific subjects.

Simple majority. One member more than half of those voting on a question.

Sine die. Adjournment without a day being set for reconvening. Final adjournment of a session of the legislature.

Speaker. Presiding officer of the assembly or house, elected by the members.

Special order. To set consideration of a bill for a specific time and day.

Status. A publication giving the status of business pending or acted upon by the legislature.

Statutes. Compilation of all the laws of a state, as passed by the legislature.

Substitute. An amendment which replaces an entire bill or resolution.

Supplemental appropriation. Adjustment of funds allocated over the original appropriation.

Suspension of the rules. A parliamentary procedure that allows actions to be taken which would otherwise be out of order. A two-thirds vote is required to suspend the rules.

Table, motion to. A means of disposing of a bill or other matter for an indefinite period of time.

Take a walk. To purposely avoid voting on a measure.

Third reading. Recitation of measure number, title, and sponsor by the reading clerk before consideration—usually final consideration.

Title. A concise statement of the contents of a bill.

Unanimous consent. Usually requested to suspend the rules for a specific purpose.

Unicameral. A legislature with one house rather than two.

Veto. The action of a governor in disapproving a measure.

Veto override. To pass a bill over the governor's veto.

Voice vote. Oral expression of the members when a question is submitted for their determination. Response is given by "ayes" and "nays" and the presiding officer states a decision as to which side prevailed.

Vote, division and rising. To vote by a show of hands or by standing.

Vote, record. A roll-call vote in which each member answers to their name and announces that he or she is voting "yea" or "nay." The vote is recorded in the journal.

Vote, roll-call. Individual votes of members are recorded in the journal.

Whip. An elected member whose duty it is to keep the rest of the members informed as to the decisions of the leadership.

Yeas and nays. Recorded vote of members on an issue. "Yea" indicates yes and "nay" indicates no.

Yield. Relinquishing of the floor by one member to another member to speak or ask a question. "Will the gentleman yield for a question?"

BIBLIOGRAPHY

• • • • • • • • •

American Society of Legislative Clerks and Secretaries and National Conference of State Legislatures. *Inside the Legislative Process*, 1992 ed. Denver: National Conference of State Legislatures, 1992.

Barber, James David. *The Lawmakers*. New Haven: Yale University Press, 1965.

Bowen, Catherine Drinker. *Miracle at Philadelphia: The Story of the Constitutional Convention, May to September 1787*. Boston: Little, Brown and Company, 1966.

Burns, John. *The Sometime Governments*. New York: Bantam Books, 1971.

California Commission on Campaign Financing. *Democracy by Initiative: Shaping California's Fourth Branch of Government*. Los Angeles: Center for Responsive Government, 1992.

"Changes in Legislative Staff." *Journal of State Government* 61 (November/December 1988).

Citizen Education Task Force of the Legislative Staff Coordinating Committee. *Educating Citizens About the Legislature: Six Recommendations*. Denver: National Conference of State Legislatures, 1993.

Congressional Quarterly. *How Congress Works*, 2nd ed. Washington, D.C.: Congressional Quarterly, 1991.

Crane, Wilder, Jr., and Meredith W. Watts, Jr. *State Legislative Systems*. Englewood Cliffs, NJ: Prentice-Hall, 1968.

Cronin, Thomas E. *Direct Democracy: The Politics of Initiative, Referendum, and Recall*. Cambridge, MA: Harvard University Press, 1989.

Council of State Governments. *The Book of the States*. Lexington, KY: Published biennially.

Dye, Thomas R. *Politics in States and Communities*, 6th ed. Englewood Cliffs, NJ: Prentice-Hall, Inc., 1988.

Ehrenhalt, Alan. "An Embattled Institution." *Governing*, January 1992.

Elazar, Daniel J. *American Federalism: A View from the States*, 3rd ed. New York: Harper & Row, 1984.

Elder, Ann H. and George C. Kiser. *Governing American States and Communities: Constraints and Opportunities*. Glenview, IL.: Scott, Foresman and Company, 1983.

Grant, Daniel R. and H. C. Nixon. *State and Local Government in America*, 3rd ed. Boston: Allyn & Bacon, Inc., 1975.

Hamilton, Alexander, John Jay, and James Madison. *The Federalist Papers*. Available in numerous editions.

Hicks, John D. *The Populist Revolt*. Minneapolis: University of Minnesota Press, 1931.

Jacob, Herbert and Kenneth N. Vines, eds. *Politics in the American States*. Boston: Little, Brown and Company, 1965.

Jewell, Malcolm E. and Samuel C. Patterson. *The Legislative Process in the United States*, 2nd ed. New York: Random House, 1973.

Jewell, Malcolm E. *The State Legislature: Politics and Practice*, 2nd ed. New York: Random House, 1962.

Jones, Rich. "State Legislatures." In *The Book of the States: 1994–95 Edition*. The Council of State Governments: Lexington, KY, 1994, pp. 98–107.

Keefe, William J. and Morris Senate Ogul. *The Legislative Process*, 6th ed. Englewood Cliffs, NJ: Prentice-Hall, 1985.

Keesey, Ray A. *Modern Parliamentary Procedure*. Boston: Houghton Mifflin, 1974.

King, Anthony, ed. *The New American Political System*, 2nd version. Washington, D.C.: AEI Press, 1990.

Kurtz, Karl T. "Changing State Legislatures." Presentation at the National Conference of State Legislatures Legislative Organization and Management Committee meeting, October 1989.

———. "The Public Standing of the Legislature." A paper prepared for the Symposium on the Legislature in the Twenty-First Century. Williamsburg, VA: National Conference of State Legislatures, March 1990.

———. "State Legislatures: Progress, Problems, and Possibilities." Eagleton Institute of Politics and National Conference of State Legislatures, draft publication, March 1992.

———. *Understanding the Diversity of State Legislatures*. Denver: National Conference of State Legislatures, 1992.

Magleby, David B. *Direct Legislation: Voting on Ballot Propositions in the United States*. Baltimore: Johns Hopkins University Press, 1984.

National Conference of State Legislatures. *Strengthening State Legislatures: A Report of NCSL's Legislative Institution Task Force*. Denver: National Conference of State Legislatures, 1994.

————. *Understanding Legislative Staff Development: A Legislator's Guide to Staffing Patterns.* Denver: National Conference of State Legislatures, 1979.

Peabody, Robert L., et al. *To Enact a Law: Congress and Campaign Financing.* New York: Praeger Publishers, 1972.

Pound, William T. "Legislatures: Dynamic Institutions." *State Legislatures,* Vol. 19, No. 1 (January 1993).

Ranney, Austin, ed. *The Referendum Device.* Washington, D.C.: American Enterprise Institute for Public Policy Research, 1981.

Rosenthal, Alan. *The Third House: Lobbyists and Lobbying in the States.* Washington, D.C.: CQ Press, 1993.

————. "Legislative Committee Systems." *Western Political Quarterly* 26 (June 1973).

————. "The Legislative Institution—Transformation and/or Decline." A paper prepared for the State of the States Symposium, Eagleton Institute of Politics, Rutgers University, December 1987.

————. *Legislative Life: People, Process, and Performance in the States.* New York: Harper & Row, 1981.

————. *Legislative Performance in the States: An Exploration of Committee Behavior.* Chicago: The Free Press, 1974.

Saffell, David C. *State and Local Government: Politics and Public Policies,* 4th ed. New York: McGraw-Hill, 1990.

Sorauf, Frank J. and Paul Allen Beck. *Party Politics in America,* 6th ed. Boston: Little, Brown and Company, 1988.

Wahlke, John C., et al. *The Legislative System.* New York: John Wiley & Sons, Inc., 1962.

Weberg, Brian. "Change Ahead for Legislative Staffs." *State Legislatures,* February 1993.

INDEX

• • • • • • • • •

by Virgil Diodato